# YOU WERE BORN PSYCHIC

## UNLOCKING YOUR ABILITIES TO CREATE YOUR BEST LIFE

Joan L. Scibienski

Flint Hills Publishing

You Were Born Psychic
Unlocking Your Abilities to Create Your Best Life
© Joan L. Scibienski 2021
All rights reserved.

Cover Design by Amy Albright

Flint Hills Publishing
**Topeka, Kansas**

www.flinthillspublishing.com

Printed in the U.S.A.

ISBN: 978-1-953583-07-9

# CONTENTS

| | |
|---|---|
| Introduction: What is Psychic Ability? | 5 |
| Vocabulary: Important Concepts Defined | 13 |
| Lesson 1: Protections and Shielding | 19 |
| Lesson 2: Creative Visualization: | |
|     Part 1 — Changing Your Life by Changing Your Thinking | 25 |
|     Part 2 — Learning to Visualize | 49 |
| Lesson 3: Guides and Angels: Learning to Contact Them | 57 |
| Lesson 4: Releasing Fear and Guilt | 67 |
| Lesson 5: Breaking Away from Judgment | 71 |
| Lesson 6: Healing Childhood Pain | 75 |
| Lesson 7: Working with Energy Part 1: Healing | 83 |
| Lesson 8: Working with Energy Part 2: Auras | 91 |
| Lesson 9: Working with Energy Part 3: Chakras | 103 |
| Lesson 10: Psychometry | 119 |
| Lesson 11: Clairvoyance | 123 |
| Lesson 12: Dreams and How to Work with Them | 131 |
| Lesson 13: Lucid Dreaming | 151 |
| Lesson 14: Astral Projection: Out-of-Body Experiences (OBE) | 155 |
| Lesson 15: Remote Viewing | 163 |
| Lesson 16: Metaphysical Tools — Introduction | 167 |
|     Tool 1: Working with a Pendulum | 167 |
|     Tool 2: Working with Crystals | 181 |
|     Tool 3: Working with Numerology | 187 |
|     Tool 4: Working with Runes | 204 |

| | |
|---|---|
| Tool 5: Working with Scrying | 206 |
| Tool 6: Working with Dowsing | 208 |
| Tool 7: Working with Cartomancy | 210 |
| Lesson 17: Spirits, Ghosts, Poltergeists | 217 |
| Lesson 18: Helping a Loved One Transition to the Other Side | 225 |
| Lesson 19: Channeling and Trance Work | 229 |
| A Final Note: Things to Consider | 235 |
| About the Author | 237 |

# INTRODUCTION

## WHAT IS PSYCHIC ABILITY?

**Many people believe that psychic ability** is either fraudulent, a special gift, a sin, demonic, or something available only to very unique people. My personal experience has proven that the ability is a survival skill that we all have. It's just that many people forget how to access it as they grow older.

*All people exhibit some form of psychic ability in their daily life.* They just aren't recognizing that they are, in fact, using their intuitive-sensing mechanism. Instead, they assign other names: *hunch, feeling, impression,* or *knowing*. Whatever you chose to call it, you are getting information in a manner inconsistent with what is happening in your physical environment. For example, you meet someone and instantaneously have a bad feeling about them. Later you might be told that they are a con artist. Or you are driving and decide for some reason to take a different route home, and later while watching the news, you discover a fatal accident happened at an intersection that you most likely would have crossed at around that same time. At the very least, that hunch saved you from being in backed-up traffic, or this feeling may have saved your life.

We survived our primitive, often dangerous beginnings by sensing when we were in danger, whether food was okay to eat, or where to go to find safety. After all, compared with lions, cobras, and bears, we should not have survived or even thrived. But we did.

As humanity became more civilized, many of these instincts were only necessary when we were in immediate danger. There are many reports of mothers knowing when their children are in danger or soldiers ducking down right before a bullet flies overhead. But becoming a civilized society meant that we created police and other authorities to keep us safe, thus we let our abilities go dormant. Like a muscle, when we work with this part of our sensing mechanism—the intuitive part—it increases in clarity and dependability.

Our intuitive muscle never vanished. It was never evil or any more special than any of our other senses are special. It is just part of our God-given human ability to prevail and continue in an often dangerous environment. Young children prior to around age three are very open to this idea. Yet, if a child sees a spirit and tells an adult, they are often told it can't be true. This can easily cause a child to shut down their psychic abilities. Older children who do continue to have metaphysical experiences may suffer tragic consequences. I have a friend whose pre-teen granddaughter was institutionalized for "hearing voices" and "seeing colors." After reading my fiction books, *The Ariana Series*, which teach metaphysical and spiritual concepts through storytelling, I am happy to report that her family now has a greater understanding that the girl is not schizophrenic, but rather, they are working to understand her psychic abilities.

Here are some of the reasons you might have shut down your abilities:

- ❖ We have others to protect us.
- ❖ Our families disapproved either due to religious beliefs, fear, or skepticism.
- ❖ You wanted to fit into a society that denies we have these abilities.
- ❖ You pride yourself on being logical and think there is no scientific way to explain this.
- ❖ You fear knowing things that you may not be able to change.
- ❖ Fear in general.

There are many terms associated with psychic phenomenon that will be explained in the definitions section of this book. To begin our discussion, however, let me explain that a "sensitive" is a person receiving psychic information. The way the information is received can vary. Some of us feel it: *clairsentience* or *empath*. Some of us hear it: *clairaudience*. Some see it: *clairvisionence* (a term I am coining because none exists). *Claircognizance* is psychic knowing. Many that are sensitive can smell things, especially when spirits are present. Others claim to be able to taste otherworldly substances. My belief is that most intuitives use a little of everything. But the most common abilities are *empath* (connecting to the mental or emotional state of another), *medium* (highly developed psychic abilities allowing connection to the Other Side), and *claircognizant*.

Psychics are known to be precognitive because they can sense a future event, or clairvoyant because they have the ability to perceive a person, object, location, and physical event through extrasensory means. These events, however, do not need to occur in the future. They can be past events, such as uncovering information about past lives, or current events, such as where to find a lost child.

A rarer occurrence within the realm of metaphysics is the psychic who can accomplish *omnipresence*, the ability to be in two or more places at the same time. If I hadn't known someone who could do this, and if there had not been evidence, I would never have believed this ability was anything but science fiction. My aunt was amazingly psychic. She predicted John F. Kennedy's assassination weeks before it happened. She didn't use her abilities for much other than family entertainment, but in the course of her life I saw her do some really awesome things. Omnipresence was one of them. She had gotten a speeding ticket that she claimed was absolutely unwarranted. She was quite angry and decided to fight the ticket. My aunt was a woman way before her time: aggressive, resolute, and unstoppable when she had her mind set on something, a true Scorpio. Reading up on the law, she came up with a strategy. The day before her court appearance she was sitting at work, reviewing her tactics over and over again in her strong mind, rehearsing for her day in court. Fellow workers came into her office and asked her questions just like any other day. The next day she arrived at the court to plead her case, and walking up to the court clerk, she presented her documents. The clerk addressed her by name and asked, "Why are you back?" Confused, my aunt asked the clerk what he meant. He told her she had pleaded her case the day before and won. He showed her the documentation to prove his assertion and even took her to talk to the judge that recognized her and addressed her by name. They also told her what she was wearing. Somehow she had been at work and won her case in court. The clothing they described was the clothing she had been wearing the day before. This was not planned. She had no idea she could do this and had never heard of omnipresence until she accomplished it. The act was completely unconscious on her part—a true out-of-body experience. My belief is that it takes a very strong mind and an extreme amount of determination to accomplish omnipresence.

*"There are more things in heaven and earth, Horatio..."* **Shakespeare**

Why did I feel the need to write this book? To me, having these abilities has enhanced my life in many ways. Death no longer frightens me and neither do those things that go "bump in the night." It has added so much depth and wonder to my everyday existence. I can help others who feel lost in their lives, as well as connect with loved ones who have died. Seeing auras and being able to work with energy helps me understand people, and by working with my own energy and aura, they respond to me more comfortably. And finally, when I listen to my guides I receive understanding, direction, guidance, safety, and knowledge. Why wouldn't you want to have all these wonderful things in your life?

More than any other reason though, is that *it is time for humanity to raise their consciousness to one of unity, love, and connection.* When we are all open to our abilities, fear is less likely to be our overriding emotion. When we begin to trust, understand, and really communicate with one another, change can begin. Opening your psychic abilities will help accomplish these goals.

Why are Mozart, Beethoven, and Bach considered superior composers and Picasso, Dali, and Leonardo di Vinci considered to be amazing artists? Because all of them listened to their inner knowing, they did not allow their abilities to frighten them, they did not allow others to convince them to abandon their gifts, and they **practiced, practiced, practiced.**

## *The Benefits You Will Receive from Studying this Book:*

I have been able to communicate with spirits since awakening from a fever-induced coma when I was seven years old. I have spent my life learning about and developing my metaphysical abilities. I have made my living for many years as a spiritual intuitive. I meet with clients, connect with their deceased loved ones and other loving entities on the Other Side, and with my academic background and years of experience in counseling, I do my best to convey the information I receive in a clear and productive manner. It is my goal to help people on this side live their best lives—the life their Soul intends for them.

Many people over the years have told me how blessed or lucky I am to have these "gifts." While I am thankful people have benefited from my skills, I am absolutely sure that the abilities I have are not unique. Every one of us can uncover our God-given abilities to see beyond the material world. You will see this theme throughout the book because it is such a fundamental concept: *You must believe in the possibility of psychic skills and then believe that you have them.*

We are living in a time when significant difficulties are facing our world. We are becoming more aware that we are no longer bounded by borders. We can be impacted by things that happen anywhere in the world. The COVID-19 pandemic is a perfect example. It started in China and within weeks was sickening people everywhere in the world. We are now a global economy which will be affected by this pandemic, too. With the internet being such an immense influence, we are becoming more alike than different and information is moving at breakneck speed whether it is truth or lies. The energies of the planet are shifting. Many people are feeling strange—they may feel unusual stress, anxiety, depression. Erratic energy can increase anger, fear, and violence. At the same time, many people are "awakening." Through this process, people realize that we are not just physical bodies but our true nature is that we are spiritual entities. Many are understanding the interconnectedness between all living things; that no one is greater than or less than another. In this process, metaphysical abilities often reappear. Many who are not aware of what is happening to them will rationalize unusual occurrences. If you haven't already, I want you to stop doing this. Instead, open your mind to the possibility that as a spiritual being, your power is limitless.

If you are open to awakening, or have begun the process, this workbook is intended to help you understand your abilities and use them properly. This will be accomplished through exercises outlined in the book. Some of the exercises you will do alone. Others should be done with a partner. I highly recommend you do the exercises in the order presented as they build on themselves. Once you become proficient with one exercise, the next one will be easier to accomplish.

Many of the exercises will include meditations. Most people when they think of meditation assume it means a complete quieting of the mind. For Eastern cultures, the concept of emptying the mind is a part of their shared cultural experience. I have come to believe this concept is so different from Western culture that it may be impossible for many people to achieve a completely quiet mind. Consequently, all I mean when I say "to meditate" is that you allow your mind to follow the directions given in the guided meditations. It will be helpful to read the meditations aloud and record them. (I believe we tend to respond best to our own voices.) You will want to do this because reading the meditation while trying to follow along with the instructions is disruptive to the process. Also, it's better to do the exercises with your eyes closed. I also recommend that the meditations be done in a sitting position: feet flat on the floor, palms facing upward on your lap. If at any time you become uncomfortable, change position. Don't think about it, just do it. If you need to scratch, scratch. And if your mind wanders, just bring it back to wherever the recording is. Make sure you are not disturbed by anything. Turn off your cell phone because even the sound of vibrating will be a distraction.

Using this workbook is not as useful as attending classes in person. But if there are no reputable classes near you, it will help with your awakening and allow you to better control what is happening to you. This workbook will not prepare you to become a professional psychic, healer, or channel. Instead, this book is designed to be used as a tool for self-awareness.

## QUESTIONS FOR FUTHER REFLCTION

**Why do I want to learn more about metaphysical subjects?**

_____
_____
_____
_____
_____
_____
_____
_____
_____
_____
_____
_____
_____
_____
_____
_____
_____
_____
_____
_____
_____
_____
_____
_____
_____
_____
_____
_____

**Am I concerned about judgment from others from studying metaphysics?**

**Do I have religious education/programming that makes me nervous about studying metaphysics?**

**Do I have someone I want to share this program of study with, working together to learn the material?**

# VOCABULARY
# IMPORTANT CONCEPTS DEFINED

**For those of you who are new** to the study of spiritual and metaphysical ideas, you may be surprised by some of the words and phrases. Some of the terms used in this context require explanation. Other terms may be completely new to you and therefore also require definition. A quick review of these words before you get started on the lessons will be helpful in your understanding of concepts we'll be exploring:

**Activation (also sometimes called ascension):** the process where a person awakens to their true nature and steps out of the fear-based, separation-based illusion. As one becomes activated, he or she becomes aware of their metaphysical abilities. During activation, a person may receive information from loving forces outside of the Earthly realm. This part of the process often occurs during sleep. If not understood, the activation process can cause disruptive energy patterns within the person. It is important to educate oneself on the process in order to deal with it effectively. An activated person comes to understand that they are creators and therefore have the ability to decide what they want to create.

**Akashic Records:** a comprehensive collection of thoughts, events, emotions, and past lives encoded in a non-physical plane of existence.

**Astral Plane:** the simplest definition is that it is a place of existence different than the material one in which we exist. It is a non-physical dimension that co-exists with our physical dimension.

**Astral Projection:** the process where the energy that is contained within our physical body leaves our body to explore a plane outside of our physical one and then returns to the body. During a projection, one may observe different planes of existence, explore past and future lives, or just explore our current world.

**Aura**: the energy field that exists around all living things. It is possible to perceive and physically feel the aura which can be made of different colors, depending on the energy of the person, and a variety of other factors.

**Clairaudience:** is a way of receiving intuitive information by hearing words, phrases, music, or other sounds. These sounds are outside the "normal" scope of hearing. They are a sort of telepathic communication from Spirit. In an emergency situation, the sound may be external.

**Clairgustance:** the ability to taste or perceive the essence of a substance from the ethereal realms without contact.

**Clairsentience:** the ability to acquire psychic knowledge by feeling.

**Clairvoyance:** the ability to perceive things or events in the future beyond normal sensory contact. Also called extrasensory perception (ESP) or sixth sense.

**Chakras:** a Sanskrit word that when translated means "wheel or disk." There are seven chakras or wheels of energy that align throughout the body, beginning at the base of the spine to the crown of the head. Many people visualize these energy centers as swirling and associate colors with the different wheels.

**Channeling (also sometimes called trance mediumship):** the ability to allow a discarnate or many discarnate entities to enter and use the physical body to communicate.

**Crystals:** are formed in nature when atoms, molecules, and ions are compressed under pressure. The process of crystal formation creates significant energy within the crystal. Different crystals have different vibrations which can be used in various metaphysical pursuits including protection and the enhancement of all variety of human emotions and physical issues.

**Divination:** the practice of seeking knowledge of the future or the unknown by supernatural means.

**Dowsing:** the ability to locate anything, including gold or silver mines, oil, but most commonly water, sometimes using a tool called a dowsing rod.

**Energy:** in the context of a spiritual discussion, "energy" refers to the life force that is within everything and also surrounds everything in the universe: from a human body to rocks buried underground. Metaphysical practitioners understand that this force comes from the Source—God.

**Equinoxx:** a collective consciousness of higher beings that are dedicated to answering questions using Joan L. Scibienski's body and mind as an unconscious channel, to share the information based on their collective knowledge, information from guides and deceased loved ones, and the Akashic Records.

**Ghosts:** an apparition of a dead person that is believed to appear or become manifest to the living. The soul of a dead person believed to be an inhabitant of the unseen world or to appear to the living in bodily likeness. Discarnate beings who have not left the physical plane.

**Hundredth Monkey:** a phenomenon in which a new behavior or idea spreads rapidly from one group to all related groups once a critical number of members of one group exhibit the new behavior or acknowledge the new idea. This is one of the fundamental spiritual principles conveyed by Equinox and is used to convey the importance in sharing spiritual knowledge to create a worldwide shift in consciousness.

**Intuition:** the ability to acquire knowledge without proof, evidence, or conscious reasoning, or without understanding how the knowledge was acquired, but instead having direct access to unconscious knowledge, unconscious cognition, inner sensing, inner insight to unconscious pattern recognition, and the ability to understand something instinctively, without the need for conscious reasoning.

**Meditation:** there are many different forms of meditation which in general means to contemplate, reflect. For a person on a spiritual path, meditation is the most effective means of connecting with the inner self, with God.

**Medium (channel):** a person with highly developed psychic abilities that connects with the Other Side. Abilities vary. Mediums may see, hear, or feel past, present, or future events. They may connect with spirits, guides, ghosts, or beings from different planes. With permission, they may access the Akashic Records. Like any profession, the skills and truthfulness of a medium should be verified by those wanting to use the medium's services.

**Omnipresence:** the ability to be present in multiple places at the same time.

**Path:** the soul's intent for a given lifetime; soul purpose.

**Poltergeist:** a noisy, usually mischievous ghost held to be responsible for unexplained noises and activities.

**Precognition (also known as premonition):** the ability to perceive future events.

**Psychic shield:** an invisible, impenetrable bubble of energy used to protect yourself from negative energy in whatever form it may take.

**Psychokinesis (or telekinesis):** the ability to manipulate objects by way of extrasensory perception.

**Reading:** takes place with a psychic advisor and is often a direct message from your guides about what you are dealing with and how to accomplish having a more successful life. Past lives and soul intent may also be explored.

**Reincarnation:** the belief that one soul experiences many different lifetimes.

**Soul:** the "true" you. The director, writer, and producer of the life you (the ego) are experiencing. The soul is our direct connection with God and is an extension of that energy.

**Spirit:** A non-quantifiable substance or energy present individually in all living things. Unlike the concept of souls (often regarded as eternal and sometimes believed to pre-exist the body), a spirit develops and grows as an integral aspect of a living being. It is a supernatural, incorporeal being.

**Spirit Guide (or guide or angels):** beings that exist on a more advanced plane of existence that are chosen to work with us to help us accomplish our soul's purpose.

**Telepathy:** the ability to transfer and receive thoughts mentally through extrasensory perception.

**Veils of Forgetfulness:** what we enter when we start a new incarnation. We forget why we are here, who we really are, and what we've done in past lives. It is there so that we can experience and learn from new perspectives without the confusion, guilt, or knowledge from past lives.

## QUESTIONS FOR FURTHER REFLECTION

**Did any of the above definitions spark a particular interest for further study?**

**Did any of the above definitions trigger any concern, even fear?**

# LESSON 1

# PROTECTIONS & SHIELDING

**Every living object** contains a force that emanates from the loving energy of God. Though it is given different names, the truth remains constant: every one of us comes from this force, and as Newton's Law of the Conservation of Energy teaches us, energy cannot be created or destroyed, it merely changes form. Spiritual people who work with their metaphysical abilities understand that our life force, our energy, comes from the source of absolute love—God. *Recognizing the existence of this powerful force is the first step in unlocking your abilities.*

Whenever we are working with our psychic abilities, our energy increases and creates a brilliant light which can be seen on all realms. (There are many more than just "Heaven" and "Earth.") Some of those realms contain spirit beings that would like to use our physical bodies in order to have substance again or some just want to mess with us. Others are angry, confused beings that can create strange, disruptive energy in our environment. Additionally, many of us that have embraced our abilities are empaths, people who pick up emotions and health problems from others we encounter. Without protection, we can be at the mercy of these random psychological emotions, physical aches and pains, and actually believe they are our own. *Consequently, I believe protections are essential for working with energy and having a healthy, happy life.*

# EXERCISE

## REMEMBER TO VISUALIZE WHITE LIGHT

There are many types of protections, some very complex and intricate, others simple. I have always preferred simple. Here is what I want you to do:

- ❖ Visualize an impenetrable White Light of Protection, like a bubble that surrounds your entire body. Imagine that anything negative bounces off this light and away from you. Ask your guides (guardian angels) and God to protect you with this White Light so that nothing can enter it that is not for your highest and best good.

- ❖ If you begin to suddenly feel sad, or if a pain appears out of the blue, ask if this is yours. If you hear *no*, ask your guides to take it away and then see your shields, the White Light, become stronger.

- ❖ Even if you can't visualize the White Light, you can imagine feeling this light surround you and know that you are safe within it. **You must absolutely believe that God's energy is the most powerful thing in the Universe and that this protection is all you need to be safe from anything.** If that belief is not there, the Light cannot do its job. Your fear will sabotage it.

Other people do more intricate protections involving crystals, prayers, salt circles, smudging, carrying a cross, or making the sign of the cross. I have never needed anything this elaborate because my belief in the White Light and God is so strong. However, if you ever feel like you are under psychic attack, take a long bath in sea salt as this is said to release negativity from the body. As you drain the tub, imagine anything negative flowing down the drain. But again, I have been involved in some unusual psychic things like ridding houses of ghosts and assisting people in releasing negative energy. Since I have started using the White Light of Protection, I have always been safe and have never had a problem.

# EXERCISE

## REMEMBER TO VISUALIZE WHITE LIGHT

*Make a List of All the Places You Should Remember to White Light*

It can be difficult to remember to cover yourself in White Light. I'm a professional psychic and sometimes even I forget! Recently, I led a ghost tour at some very active places. You can be sure I covered myself and the tour participants in White Light. But at an open house for my books, with many people coming and going, I completely forgot! So, make a list to help remind you to cover yourself and others in White Light. Keep the list in a place where you will see it. Here are a few examples to get your started:

~ Driving in your car. *I have a mantra: "I ask that the car and all within it be surrounded with God's White Light of Protection. Help us to get where we go and back safely and with no problems, and thank you for all the help you've been giving me."*

~ Entering your work place.

~ Entering a store, restaurant, another's home.

~ List Additional Places:

___
___
___
___
___
___
___
___
___
___
___
___
___
___
___

I've admitted there are times and places I've forgotten to shield. That's normal. However, if your mood shifts dramatically, or if you feel sick or have a sudden pain, remember most likely you are picking up something that is in your environment. Release it by thanking your guides and asking them to take it away, and then tighten your shielding.

No matter how long you have been working with your abilities, you can be vulnerable. Don't let it scare you. Instead, ask your guides for help to remove the unwanted feelings and they will.

# MEDITATION

BEFORE YOU BEGIN YOUR MEDIATION, RECORD IT IN YOUR OWN VOICE.

Seat yourself comfortably in a well-lit room. Close your eyes and breathe deeply. As you breathe, feel your body relax. Visualize a clear quartz crystal. Look deeply into the clear depth of the crystal. Feel yourself surrounded by this crystal as though you are in a transparent bubble of crystalline white light. See the crystal as being permeable for wonderful gifts from God and your guides, but completely closed to anything else. Feel the warmth and safety inherent in being deep within this wonderful White Light of Protection. Then in your mind think, *I am surrounded and protected within this wonderful light of protection; God's White Light of Protection. Nothing can harm me here. I am safe, I am strong, and I am completely protected. Thank you, God.* Breathe the feeling of safety and connection to this pure form of love, light, and goodness. After a few minutes of becoming familiar with this complete feeling of safety, understand that all you need to be completely safe in any situation is to visualize this crystal of light. Ask God and the guides to protect you and keep out anything that isn't essential to your better health and safety. Now—begin to count up from one to five and feel yourself coming back into the here and now feeling great, much better than before.

# REFLECTION

**Are you remembering to practice protections? If not, what could you do to remind yourself?**

_____
_____
_____
_____
_____
_____
_____
_____
_____

*A Suggestion* — Put a crystal in your car and bedroom so that they will be a reminder. If you are having difficulty with the crystal visualization, try to hold the image of the crystal for longer periods of time. However, if you feel as though you are forcing yourself, then gradually increase the time you visualize the crystal. The quality of the visualization is very important. Over time it will be easier. Just like a weight-lifting program, start off slowly and be patient.

**What have you experienced during the meditation exercise?**

_____
_____
_____
_____
_____
_____
_____
_____
_____
_____
_____
_____
_____

Don't be disappointed if you found it hard to visualize. It will come to you eventually. Here is a way I have helped my clients to understand visualization: *Pretend you are daydreaming*. Visualization works exactly the same way.

If you don't remember anything and think you fell asleep, you may actually have been in a deep meditation. If this happened, you will have awakened when you were told to, feeling fine, wide awake, better than before. If you *did* fall asleep, do these meditations earlier in the day when you are less likely to be tired.

# LESSON 2
## CREATIVE VISUALIZATION PART 1: CHANGING YOUR LIFE BY CHANGING YOUR THINKING

Thoughts are things. I am sure you have heard that statement more than once. But what does that really mean? In a nutshell: *What we think and believe is what we become.*

There are several reasons to examine your beliefs, but the two that are most relevant to this book are: *You must examine how your beliefs may hinder the development of your abilities.* And if your life is out of control or unhappy: *Helping to empower your mind will help to create a better life.* When you have the security you need, you can work more diligently on becoming more spiritual.

When we dwell on all that is wrong or that could go wrong with our lives, we create a life filled with fear and worry. Every day becomes a struggle as we envision all the possible negative scenarios that could befall us.

Thoughts are energy and as such they can help draw to us more negative energy. In interviews with serial rapists, the FBI Behavioral Analysis Unit discovered that rapists picked their prey because of a vibration the person exhibited. The rapists claimed that certain women stood out as victims while others did not. When we surround ourselves with negative thoughts, we draw negative energy, creating a potential of becoming a victim. Consequently, with each real or imagined victimization we more firmly and concretely align ourselves with negativity, creating a pattern and a circle of pain and fear.

Even more insidious is that many of us have been programmed as children to believe in adverse ways. Those beliefs were implanted in our subconscious minds prior to our rational brains having been formed. Accepted as truth without examination, we continue to let these "truths" control our behavior without really looking to see if they are relevant to what we want in our lives now. Religious beliefs are an example of this. All of us have heard of "religious guilt," but there are many other ways we are programmed.

Socrates claimed that an unexamined life is not worth living. I contend unexamined beliefs are what create much of our pain, fear, limitations, and failures. To move beyond our cycles of victimization, we must first discover what our real beliefs are.

*Merriam-Webster Dictionary* defines fear as "an unpleasant often strong emotion caused by expectation or awareness of danger." Certainly, we all must be aware of danger in our lives, but think of all the times you feared that something or someone was harmful without basing that fear on actual proof. Most of this fear is programmed into you either through what you have been told or what you picked up by the responses of those around you.

I had a deep dislike of cats until my 20s, when a kitten adopted me. At first I reacted hostilely to it. But being a cat, it was intrigued by anyone that didn't think it was just wonderful and she kept pursuing me. She wouldn't leave me alone, and eventually, she won my heart. Through this interaction, I was encouraged to examine my negative convictions about cats. Where had they come from? Why did I react to them fearfully and hatefully? What about them was so terrible? I loved animals, why were cats different for me? Was it due to a past life? Through meditation I became aware that it was a learned behavior caused by a childhood experience. When my mother was young, she witnessed a frightening experience involving a cat which caused her to view them as dirty, horrifying creatures. She would respond fearfully to them any time she was near one. I remembered a particularly intense experience when I was a very small child, a curious toddler. I was on a walk with my mother when we came across a kitten. I remember reaching for it. Immediately, my mother forcefully grabbed me, dragging me away. There were no words exchanged, but the fear and hatred radiated from her, causing me to become fearful and judgmental of cats, too. I had never taken the time to ascertain why I responded negatively to them, there was no need as I just stayed away from them. But how many other, less obvious things are defining my judgments, fears, and pain that create the life I am living?

A core belief is one that is so basic to the way you think, believe, and conduct your life that you never stop to think about them. You take the belief for granted and operate from it automatically.

## What are Your Core Beliefs?

There are five categories of core beliefs:

1. **Self-responsibility** — victim or growth?
   Powerless, helplessness, confusion or empowerment?

2. **Self-esteem** — how do you see yourself?
   Powerful, beautiful, accomplished or ugly and worthless?

3. **Trust in the Universe** — victim or supported?
   Life is working or nothing ever works out for you?

4. **Positive Attitude** — how do you feel about challenges, your life, and your future? Do you see the good in most things or see the aphids instead of the roses?

5. **Change** — flow or block? Resist new things or flow with whatever comes?

The Universe abhors holes. Have you ever noticed that if you dig a hole at the beach or in your yard, within no time something fills it, whether it's water, dirt, or sand. It's the same with people. Create holes in your past belief system by weeding out negative or dysfunctional programming so that you can fill the holes with new thoughts, goals, and beliefs.

You can change your core beliefs. The great psychotherapist Karl Menninger stated, "Fears are educated into us, and can, if we wish, be educated out." So can any programming if you take the time to do the work. It is time to reprogram your thinking so that you can take control and empower your life.

This is a lengthy but important exercise consisting of three basic steps:

**Step 1: Examine your thinking to discover your core beliefs.**

**What are you afraid of and why?**

**Are your fears logical and based on facts, not just on what you've been told?**

**Do you believe you are powerful?**

**List what helps you feel safe and powerful:**

**List what makes you feel uncomfortable and powerless:**

**What has religion taught you? Is this belief empowering and does it help you to feel you have control over your life?**

**What do you think about women? Why?**

**What do you think about men? Why?**

**What do you believe about sex? Why?**

**What does happiness look like to you?**

## What controversial beliefs do you hold and why?

## What do you believe about psychic ability?

**What do you believe about channeling and trance work?**

**What do you believe about death?**

**What do you believe about money or success and successful people?**

**If you are brave,** a wonderful way of learning about yourself is to ask five or more friends and relatives to describe how they see you. This can teach you quite a bit about your own beliefs and subconscious. Do not lead them—just let them talk about who you are. Don't respond, just thank them, and then later, think about what they said. Ask them to discuss (from their point of view) what they thought about your answers to the questions in this exercise. See where there are differences.

# REFLECTION

**Examine your thinking**—especially anything that causes fear, anger, or sadness. Weed out the garden of your programmed beliefs. If you say you want a good relationship but you don't believe in them, then you will manifest your true belief. You will reinforce your fear and doubt and never reach your goal of loving and being loved.

If you resent people with wealth and success, then the negative energy around that resentment will translate into repelling your own success and wealth. If you should achieve prosperity anyway, it will bring you distress instead of happiness, or you will lose it again. There are many stories of lottery winners who are bankrupt within a year.

## Step 2: What you need to begin to create your new way of thinking.

*Desire—you must completely want to change your life and empower yourself.*

**Why do you want change?**
_____
_____
_____
_____
_____
_____
_____
_____

**What might you have to give up if your life changes?**

**How will your life feel, look, and be when you take control of your thinking?**

*Belief is Key!*
*You must completely believe you can do this, you want to do this, and you are prepared to do what it takes to accomplish it.*

**What could stop you?**

**What got in the way of believing in yourself in the past?**

**How might your family and friends get in your way? How could they support your efforts?**

_____
_____
_____
_____
_____
_____
_____
_____
_____
_____
_____
_____
_____
_____
_____
_____
_____
_____

*Acceptance is Critical!*
*You must accept that you are worthy of accomplishing anything you desire and put your mind toward your goal. You must accept that you can do it—no doubts.*

**What could get in your way of accepting?**

_____
_____
_____
_____
_____
_____
_____
_____
_____
_____
_____
_____
_____
_____

**In what areas of your life do you consider yourself unworthy?**

**Why do you feel you deserve the things you are programming over someone else?**

## Step 3: Goal Setting.

Decide on something that you want to achieve. Make the description as detailed as possible: smell, taste, colors, feelings. Make your first goal small and manageable enough to succeed. You will do better when you have had some successes. If you start big and don't succeed right away, you will give up. Define the goals and the steps. Do you feel yourself doing these things? If not, what do you need to work on to get ready? If you have trouble visualizing, make a vision board. Clip pictures and words from magazines that relate to your goal. Put them somewhere you will see them often. Look at them and say to yourself, "This or something better is manifesting perfectly in my life right now and this is true!" Saying positive phrases throughout the day reaffirming your acceptance of achieving your goals is also helpful if *you truly believe what you are saying*. If you don't feel worthy, then these affirmations will not help.

Below are some example goals that may or may not be appropriate for you. Use them as a guide:

### Week 1 Goal: Spend a day pampering myself.

(It is important to practice self-care, particularly if you are an empath. Otherwise you will drain your energy and become negative or unhealthy.)

**What can you do to pamper yourself?**

_____
_____
_____
_____
_____
_____

**Imagine how it will feel:**

_____
_____
_____
_____
_____
_____

**If need be, how will you begin to put money away to accomplish this goal without guilt?**

___

      Goal 2: Make a larger goal for one month. Go on a weekend trip.

**What kind of trip? See it clearly.**

___

**How much money will it cost?**

___

**Make reservations if necessary.**

### Goal 3: A year from now, buy a new car.

**Pick out the car and describe it fully.**

**Take a test drive and feel yourself owning and driving it daily. Focus on this vision often. Describe the experience. What does it feel like?**

**Tell everyone your plan to buy the car and start saving. How does making this overt commitment make you feel?**

### Goal 4: Five-year or ten-year plan: have a successful career.

**What can you see yourself doing and loving for the rest of your life?**

**What training do you need to accomplish this goal?**

**What information do you need to accomplish the goal?**

_____
_____
_____
_____
_____
_____
_____
_____
_____
_____
_____
_____

# REFLECTION

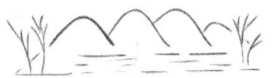

**These are all hypothetical examples of goals you might consider.** Remember—do everything in bite-sized steps. If you attempt to accomplish too much too fast you will cause yourself to fail. Never diet, quit smoking, and change jobs all at the same time. If you succeed, it will be wonderful and amazing, but if you fail, you will lose your belief in your ability to succeed. However, if you sabotage yourself it is a wonderful opportunity to look at your old programming and begin the work of changing it.

You may find that you have problems feeling guilty when you get what you want. Many women, for example, have a fear of success. Examine the guilt so that you can move past the underlying programming. Consider how wonderful it feels to be generous with success either by helping others less fortunate or teaching others to succeed.

Listen for old **lack programming**: *It's a sin to have too much. Life is hard then you die. Who are you to think you deserve that? It's lonely at the top. Filthy rich.* Those words and thoughts mean nothing unless you accept that they mean something to you. Contradict them with positive, reinforcing thoughts like: *The world is filled with more than enough for everyone to be happy, successful, and safe. I live in an* *abundant, safe, loving world. I am a wonderful, giving person, and I allow prosperity to be part of my life.*

Very often when we begin to change, our families and friends will seem to go out of their way to defeat us. It's not that they do not love us, it's because if we succeed they will feel forced to examine why they are choosing to remain stuck. Change is difficult and often scary and most people will not even start on the path, while others sabotage their success and feel worse when they watch someone else succeed. Also, when we change, those around us are forced to change somewhat to continue to relate to us. People may complain about the status quo, but many are afraid to take the steps to change it. Love them without judgment, but keep moving forward with your plan.

*Gratitude is one of the best ways to tell the Universe you are ready for more wonderful things.* By being grateful for all the things you already have, you are creating the energy of abundance in your life. Even if you don't think you have anything to be grateful for, when you begin to put together an inventory you will see you have a lot more than you recognized. Each of us has the ability to create and that in itself is magic. We live on a beautiful planet with air to breathe, water to drink, and grass to lie on. Most of us have some shelter, food, and a physical body that is usable. That's a beginning we can all build upon.

# CREATIVE VISUALIZATION PART 2: LEARNING TO VISUALIZE

**Visualization is a mental image or picture** of what you want to create in your life. It is a technique involving focusing on positive mental images to achieve a goal. Visualization does not require special skills. It is a process of creativity and imagination rather than an optical technique.

To visualize, you need to think of an image that represents what you want. If it is a car, what does it look like? What year, make, color, and style is it? Get as clear a picture in your mind as possible. If the vision evokes a feeling it will be more powerful. Put yourself in the picture. See yourself happily enjoying it. See yourself sitting behind the wheel and feel all the excitement of showing it off to your friends and family. Focus on this vision often, each time feeling the joy of having manifested your desire.

**What do you want to manifest? Describe it in detail.**

_____
_____
_____
_____
_____
_____
_____
_____
_____
_____
_____
_____
_____
_____
_____
_____
_____
_____
_____
_____

_____
_____
_____
_____
_____
_____
_____
_____
_____
_____
_____
_____
_____
_____
_____
_____

As you achieve your worldly goals you will become more secure and empowered; you will believe in yourself. This will make developing your abilities easier and help you to be confident and accomplished enough to help others. Giving back to the Universe creates abundance for all of us.

## Using a Vision Board

This can be a fun activity and works especially well for those who are still having problems with visualization.

Either get your hands on some magazines or go to images on the internet. Think of what you want to manifest. For instance, if you are programming a great relationship, begin looking for pictures of couples that are intimate, loving, and connected. Either cut out or print these pictures. If it is a car, find pictures of the car. This is even more effective if you can find the exact color.

After procuring the pictures, either paste them in a scrapbook, put them up all over your house (especially on the mirror you use to get yourself ready every morning), or attach them to a posterboard or cork board.

The idea is that every time you look at the pictures, you allow yourself to feel yourself in the car, the relationship, the house, new job, or whatever you are working to manifest. It is a daily reminder of what you are working on and what you can have. It is a statement to the Universe that you are sincere in this desire, you are clear on what you want, and you are willing to do the work to achieve this goal.

# Using Affirmations

Affirmations are the conversion of your positive thoughts into phrases you recite to yourself to reinforce your visualizations and changing patterns of thought. This means you must be very careful with your words, choosing to speak only those that work for your benefit and the cultivation of your highest good. Affirmations help purify your thoughts and restructure your brain so that you truly begin to think nothing is impossible for you.

Always use positive language in your affirmations and put them in the present, not the future. Write them down. They have more impact that way. Be succinct and specific. It must be about yourself, not about changes you want to see in someone else.

*Examples of affirmations:*

- I can accomplish anything!
- I am so proud of all I have accomplished!
- I have a wonderful life right now!
- I am financially abundant.
- I am exceptionally healthy.
- My weight is in perfect proportion to my body.

If your visualizations, positive thoughts, and affirmations don't manifest what you want, you will need to look at your core beliefs again to determine if this is *really* what you want and determine if there is any old programming that may be sabotaging your success. Try asking yourself these questions:

**Are there still uncleared, deeply-held beliefs that run contrary to your affirmations?**

_____
_____
_____
_____
_____
_____
_____
_____
_____

**Is this something you really want or just think you should want?**

**Is the world conducive to what you want to manifest, or would it be better to wait?**

## Could the timing be wrong?

## Are you afraid?

## Will it create a major change in your life that you are not ready for?

# What fear could it be activating?

**One of the most fun ways I say my affirmations is to sing them.** While driving somewhere, cleaning house, or whenever you are—sing along to music, change the words, and insert your affirmation. Music creates feeling, and adding real feeling to any affirmation gives it much more power. It allows you to use your creativity by making the new lyrics fit the song. Enjoy!

*"The most powerful thing you can do to change the world, is to change your own beliefs about the nature of life, people, reality, to something more positive…and begin to act accordingly."* Shakti Gawain

# LESSON 3

# GUIDES AND ANGELS: LEARNING TO CONTACT THEM

**Guides are people on the astral plane** that the soul chooses to help the ego through a particular lifetime. They are not loved ones who have passed. They are not tied to you in this lifetime except by their commitment to help you succeed. I believe they are people we have interacted with in past lives that are committed to helping us with our path in our current life. They are similar to our best friends; they want us to be happy and they will advise us in ways so we can master our life to accomplish our life's mission. We just have to listen for their communication to us. Often we mistake their advice for our own intuition. But if you spend any time getting to know your guides, you will discover they talk to us about things we are not even thinking about and they also sound quite different than our inner voices.

Your guides can help with problem solving. They help provide direction to get you on your path. They help teach about spiritual growth and they can protect you. They are excellent about warning us if we are off path or about to do something troubling. They also work with us to help with our psychic growth.

Most people don't realize their guides are talking to them because most of us don't listen to our inner voices. Your guide is the voice you hear when you're about to walk into traffic and you hear, "Don't!" then find yourself jumping back, barely avoiding being hit by a driver who is turning without looking. One of my clients recently told me about an experience she had on vacation with her husband and small sons at Disney World. While stepping from a grassy area onto the lane in front of her hotel, a huge bus came at a fast speed around the corner. She heard that inner voice telling her to, *Move!* If she hadn't listened, she feels certain she would have been flat as a Mickey Pancake! Or when you meet someone new and you hear, *Be careful of this person*. That's your guides giving you a warning. The realization that you were warned usually happens after the event because most of us are not listening.

There are many ways you can enlist the help of your guides. The easiest way is through meditation. Begin your meditation with the intent of meeting one of your guides, of talking with them. Set a time every day for this meditation, preferably the same time, and make sure you are not disturbed. Wear comfortable clothing. Sit in the position I discussed earlier: feet on the floor, palms of your hands facing up. Put yourself at "level"—a state of relaxation—by breathing then counting downward from 10 to 1, then wait. At some point you will realize the voices going through your mind have changed. The voices are not berating you, or thinking about your day, or telling you that you have better things to do. These voices will begin to talk with you about concerns or they will start giving you instructions. It could take weeks before you realize you are hearing something other than your own thoughts or, for some people, it could take minutes. Your progress depends on what preconceived notions you have about your abilities and how distractible you are.

For some, their guides appear in their mind's eye, giving them clear impressions or visions of what a particular guide looks like. If you are religious, the guide may appear as Jesus, Mary, or an angel. One of my clients had guides that looked like Mickey and Minnie Mouse! When asked why they took this form, they replied that they knew he loved Mickey and Minnie and would feel secure working with them in that guise. *Because guides are energy, they can take any form that you will relate to, even animal forms. However, they will never take the form of anything that scares you.*

Guides are with you from birth, but not all of them work with you at the same time. Consequently, at any one time you may have two or more working with you depending upon how difficult your life is at the time, whether you are beginning something new, working on some particular karma or path, or have asked for specific guides to work with you. There will always be at least two, one male and one female, but there is no set number of guides each person can have. The notion of male and female guides refers to their essence as well as their appearance.

Obviously, the guides that are with you when you are four years old will not be the same ones that are there when you are 35. You have different needs and requirements. And hopefully you will be working on different things. Each guide helps you with various areas of your life and your learning. One may be there to help with career, another to encourage fun, the Gatekeeper Guide is useful as you work more with other realms, and yet another will help with relationships. You will also have a Master Guide. This is the entity that helps with your spiritual growth. This is the guide that doesn't answer questions, but teaches by asking you questions. Great growth can happen when you are working with your master guide.

Recently I was made aware of another type of guide or master. They are called Soul Keepers because they can convey and work with you on mastering and understanding your soul's intent for this life and the path that you are meant to walk. I was given this new information to help the many seekers who are becoming activated, opening up to their natural psychic abilities, and are craving answers to why they are here, especially at this critical time on our planet.

There are many ways people connect with their guides: sweat lodges, vision quests, deprivation, drugs. But these extremes are not necessary unless you believe they are. I've found just trusting and listening works well. Below are some suggested exercises to help you get started on the important and rewarding journey of meeting your guides. I can assure you that your guides are thrilled you are trying to hear them.

# EXERCISE

REMEMBER TO
## VISUALIZE WHITE LIGHT

### Hand Position to Call to Your Guides

A trick I learned in a course I took some years ago is to put your thumb, index finger, and middle fingers together. Mentally ask a question and listen to the immediate answer. It will be from your guides. *For this technique, you must have an agreement with your guides that you will be using this practice for immediate answers only.* For example, use it to ask questions like: is this food safe to eat? Should I turn right or left to get to my destination? Am I safe here?

# MEDITATION

BEFORE YOU BEGIN YOUR MEDIATION,
RECORD IT IN YOUR OWN VOICE.

Relax, breathe, and when focused, begin the countdown from ten to one. This time visualize or feel yourself descending an ancient, marble staircase. Allow yourself to feel the cool stone under your bare feet. Feel the moisture in the air as you descend, and notice as the air gets cooler. Tell yourself that with each step downward, you are getting deeper and deeper within yourself. Remind yourself to relax, release, and go deeper and deeper. When you reach the number one, the bottom step, find yourself in a crystal cavern; floor and ceiling covered in crystal. Notice the colors that are radiated from the prisms within the crystals. Now you see a path walking through the crystals. Begin to walk along this path, secure and filled with anticipation. In your mind, ask your guides to make themselves known to you.

Allow yourself to hear a sound in the distance; the sound of running water. Walk toward the sound as you feel the moisture in the air increase. As you round a corner, you see a pool of water which draws you toward its dark, hypnotic surface. You have a strong desire to bend down and stare into the water. As you look into this mirror-like pool, you see your face staring back at you, but there is also another face or two. See yourself sit down and continue staring into the water as you adjust yourself to the features and the feel of this other being. When you are comfortable, turn around and greet them. Ask for names. This is the time to suggest the clasped thumb and pointer finger technique you have learned and ask if they will also work with your pendulum.

When you become comfortable with this guide or guides, it is time to come back to the here and now. Thank them for being here for you and begin to count up from one to five. At number three, begin to feel your body becoming alive. At four, your consciousness is back sitting in the room you started the meditation in, and at five, find yourself wide awake feeling great, so much better than before.

## QUESTIONS FOR FURTHER REFLECTION

**Have you established a time in your day that you will meditate and reach out to your guides? What can you do to make this a routine?**

**Record your experiences during your meditation. Have you received impressions, names, messages?** *(It is very important to keep detailed notes whenever possible. As more information is revealed, it will be difficult to remember what you are learning.)*

Joan L. Scibienski

*Do not be disappointed if you don't see a guide right away.* You have spent many years not acknowledging them so it can take a while for you to connect. Keep working on it. One of the ways I have suggested to clients is right before they fall asleep at night, ask for a guide to come during a dream. If you remember your dreams, you will usually within a week or two recognize that you have had a dream where you were talking with someone or something. That's the guide. Remember they can appear as anything, even someone you know.

If you don't remember your dreams, during the day affirm your desire to meet a guide and keep meditating and allowing them to come to you in that way.

Many of my clients ask how they know that they are actually working with a guide instead of it being a regular dream or their imagination. The only way you will know is by getting to know this entity. If it is just a dream it would be very rare for it to continue—to stop at a particular place one night and continue on the next like a serialized novel. Additionally, if you are getting information that is valuable or answering a question you have been contemplating, and that information is coming in a conversation within the dream, then it is likely you are communicating with a guide.

My guides have a different way of speaking and also often interject things into my mind I haven't been thinking about. Usually whatever they are telling me to do or to examine ends up being quite relevant for me.

Until you are used to using your abilities, you will question everything, and that's really not a bad thing. Testing yourself is healthy. But you need to get out of your way by not trying to rationalize or explain what you are getting through "logical thinking." Psychic phenomenon is rarely logical or easily explained. Most people aren't happy hearing, "I just feel it." They desire more precise answers. *Sometimes you must just trust and let time reveal whether your intuition was correct or not.*

## Contacting Your Guides Through Automatic Writing

Contacting your guides through meditation can be harder for some people than others. I have suggested to some of my clients that they use a technique called automatic writing. This is the practice of bringing forth information from your guides, higher consciousness, or your subconscious mind without consciously writing. It is another way to channel information.

The actual procedure is easy. The most difficult part is to have your mind focus on something else and get out of the way. *Do not analyze anything, just do it.*

**Procedure:**

- Seat yourself in a chair next to a table or at your computer.
- Have a piece of paper and a writing implement on the table or your hands on the computer keyboard.
- Protect yourself.
- State your intent and ask your guides and angels for help.
- Relax and breathe.
- Think of or write down a question.
- Just let your mind wander or listen to music or watch a video.
- Pay no attention to your hand.
- If you need a nudge to get started, just start writing whatever enters your mind.

It's that simple. At some point, you will either receive an answer to your question or some type of communication. If nothing happens, try again the next day.

**Reasons to learn automatic writing:**

- To contact your guides.
- To get answers to questions.
- To reach your subconscious mind.
- To work on a new way to receive information from other sources.

❖ To create. I believe I channeled *The Ariana Series*, especially the first book, *Be the Light*, because it seemed to flow out of me without me even thinking.

# EXERCISE

### REMEMBER TO
## VISUALIZE WHITE LIGHT

**After you've acquired a blank journal for your automatic writing practice, seat yourself and ask this question:** *What can I do to increase my abilities?*

# LESSON 4

# RELEASING FEAR AND GUILT

**Releasing fear and guilt are ongoing processes** throughout our lifetimes. To quote Shrek, "We are like onions, many layered." Here are some techniques that have worked for me, starting with the simple and going to the more difficult:

### Releasing Guilt:

**Take stock of what you did.** Determine what you learned from what you did and decide you will never repeat that act again, then—LET IT GO.

**Examine what you are getting** from holding onto the guilt. Is it attention? Martyrdom? Excuses for not moving forward in your life? Can you get these things in any other way?

**Look at whether the guilt is warranted.** Often, we are programmed early in our lives with rules that are guilt-producing. For example, when we are twelve-year-old females we are warned against indiscriminate sex and that we will be looked at as "bad" if we are sexual at that age. That same sexual guilt can follow us the rest of our lives. In our early teens, the sanctions may be somewhat warranted, but they are not later in life. This is just one example of rules that can follow us, and if left unexamined, can create guilt and shame. Examine your guilt and decide if it has any true relevance for your current life. Release with love that which is no longer relevant and move into the present. It is also essential to realize that if something was done to you—rape or abuse, for example—*it was not your fault. Release this guilt so you will stop being victimized.*

### Releasing Fear:

Fear is a bit more complex and insidious. Some fear exists from past lives, but many fears are cultural, situational, or learned. Fear of using your psychic abilities is often due to religious programming or learned fears passed down by a parent or someone important in our lives. Many fears are passed down from parent to child without one word being spoken. Prejudice can be an example of this. A parent may not even realize they have a fear of a certain religious, ethnic, or racial group, but when they are near someone that fits that mold, they hold the child's hand tighter or walk faster. This sends a message of fear to that impressionable child.

**All fears must be examined**. It is too easy to let them go untested and thus they rule our lives.

**Ask yourself when the first time you experienced this fear was**. If you can't remember, attempt to figure it out through meditation. Go to your "meditative laboratory" (as I will show you in the following meditation) and focus on the fear. Allow the feelings to come to the surface.

**Know that you are safe**. Allow yourself to see what the absolute worst thing that could happen would be, then see what you would do if it did. See yourself win!

**Another technique is to see your fear playing on a screen in front of you**. Keep reminding yourself that you are watching it—*it is not happening to you*. Allow the screen to move farther and farther away as you are watching it. Feel the fear also move farther and farther away.

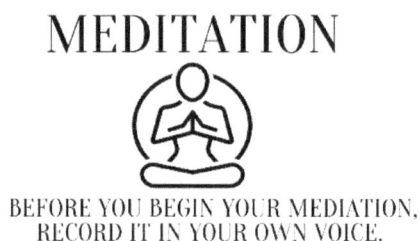

## -Laboratory Meditation-

Make yourself comfortable, feet on the floor, back straight, in a safe place. Breathe deeply: in-and-out, in-and-out, in-and-out. Keep breathing and relax. With each inhalation of breath, feel yourself going deeper within. With each exhalation of your breath, feel yourself relaxing, releasing, releasing, and becoming calm. Deeper and deeper, relax, release, calm. Keep this up for several minutes.

Now, begin counting down from ten to one, and with each descending number, feel yourself going deeper and deeper within. Ten, deeper and deeper. Nine, even deeper now. Eight, when you reach the number one you will be ten times deeper or 100 times deeper if you so desire. Relax and go deeper now. Seven, relax, relax and go deeper. Six, five, four, deeper and deeper relaxed. Ten times deeper or 100 times more relaxed. Three, when you reach one you will be completely relaxed and at peace, completely relaxed. Two, one, 100 times deeper than you were before.

Before you is an ancient door. It is made of carved wood with ancient writing and runes engraved in it, and as you reach to touch it, it opens. You walk into a massive room. At one end is a large screen exactly like you would see in a movie theatre. There is also a desk with a complete top-of-the-line computer system, a wall of ancient books that contain all the knowledge of the world, and a laboratory that contains everything you need to heal yourself and others. This is your *laboratory level of the mind*; the level you can visit to accomplish anything. Here you can solve any problem, heal yourself and others, and do anything you can think of. All you need to do to get back to this mind-level is to have the intent to come to this level of the mind and count down from ten to one.

At this level of the mind, there will always be at least one of your guides present. It is time to meet this guide. You will have time now to talk with this guide. Learn their name and how to contact them in the future. *(Give yourself several minutes for this conversation.)*

It's time to come back now. I'm going to count from one to five and when I reach five you will be wide awake and back to this time and place. Wide awake feeling great, better than before. One, two, coming up slowly. Three, feel a cool breeze bathing your face. Four, your toes and fingers tingling and coming awake now. Five, wide awake feeling wonderful.

***Here's an additional suggestion.*** Years ago, I participated in a personal growth workshop. During this workshop, we were challenged to face a fear. From as far back as I could remember, I had a phobia of spiders which was made worse when I was bitten by a Brown Recluse. Because of the facilitator's encouragement, I went to a pet shop and held a Tarantula. It took me a bit of time to build up my courage, but I did it! I felt incredibly empowered. I would love to see each of you explore a fear and conquer it. Don't do anything dangerous, but find a fear, and if you can safely challenge it, do it. With each success you have, the greater your confidence will become.

# LESSON 5

# BREAKING AWAY FROM JUDGMENT

**For those that are on a spiritual journey**, it is to critical stop judging others. Our current social media-driven culture can make this difficult. But we must step back and realize: **we are all one.** There is no room for racism, sexism, homophobia, or judgment of any type. This lesson contains a meditation to help you release any vestige of judgment.

Throughout life we may meet others that we either automatically dislike, or perhaps through our interactions with them, we grow to dislike them due to specific behaviors. This can make our lives uncomfortable, especially if this is a co-worker, boss, or family member. This meditation is designed to help you to grow beyond the dislike and learn to change your thinking.

# MEDITATION

BEFORE YOU BEGIN YOUR MEDIATION, RECORD IT IN YOUR OWN VOICE.

### -Meditate to Release Judgment-

Make yourself comfortable in a room where you will not be disturbed for at least 20 minutes. Sit comfortably, feet flat on the floor. Begin to breathe deeply. Focus on your breath, noticing the ebb and flow while relaxing your body and mind. Counting down from ten to one slowly, allow your body and mind to relax even more deeply with each descending number. When you reach the number one, feel yourself to be deeply relaxed. Begin to visualize the face of a person with whom you are having difficulty. Just see the face. Attach no emotions to what you are seeing. Allow yourself to imagine what life must be like for this person. Attempt to visualize them as children. See their family life, their schooling, and their friendships. Pay attention to what they desire, fear, and need. Like you, they want to feel safe, loved, and happy. Allow yourself to understand and feel that every human is the same with the same desires and the same fears. What makes us different are the ways in which we have responded to the experiences of our lives. We all crave love and acceptance, but if this was not received in childhood, then many people become bitter or withdrawn, and even bullies who ultimately push others away. Or they may become pleasers or drama queens or martyrs. We are the same—what's different is how we react to our experiences and how we perceive them. Feel the connections instead of focusing on what appears to be different. When next you see the people, you may see them differently. If not, allow yourself to remember your connection and your awareness of who they really are. Often this will solve the issues between you.

## QUESTIONS FOR FURTHER REFLECTION

**Think about what you were told as a child about other religious groups. Pick one that has a particularly strong charge to it and read up on their religious beliefs. How does that map into what you were told? How does that old belief effect how you look at people that belong to that religion even now?**

___
___
___
___
___
___
___
___
___
___
___
___
___
___

**Spend some time at a homeless shelter or working with the homeless. Find out what brought them to this situation. What did you learn by being around them? How could that situation happen to anyone?**

_____

Much of our judgment about things or people come from our families, peer groups, society. Most of the people or groups of people we reject are those we have never really been involved with in any real way. We don't really know them. ***Keep challenging yourself to walk in another person's shoes.*** Are there certain types of people or groups that you judge? If so, get to know some. Go to their gatherings, reach out on social media. Find a way to connect and to talk with people. You have nothing to lose.

# LESSON 6

# HEALING CHILDHOOD PAIN

**Many of us, if not all of us,** have had a variety of challenges while growing up. Even if we don't consciously realize it, there may be some unresolved hurt at the level of our subconscious. Humans are excellent at *stuffing* or refusing to deal with pain, so it festers inside of us, often causing both emotional and physical problems.

Pain must be acknowledged. It will not go away on its own. Avoidance of pain actually increases it. Allow yourself to really look at it, grieve, and talk with others about it, if you can. Unresolved deep pain always brings out emotional demons like bitterness, victimhood, or self-blame and hatred.

Make a decision to let go. If you resist letting it go, you must examine what the pain is giving you that you can't live without. Could it be attention? Or is it that you now identify so completely with helplessness that you are afraid to take back your power?

In every moment you have a choice: to continue to feel bad about another person's actions or to take back your power from them and start feeling good.

There is a belief among some native people that when you are abused, the abuser takes a piece of your soul and replaces it with a piece of their severely damaged one. The only way to be whole is to forgive the perpetrator, thus removing the diseased chard and replacing it with healing.

Forgiveness is not easy. It is downright hard. But it is essential to letting go of pain and moving forward from the past into a much brighter future. You do not have to forgive the act perpetrated on you, but you must let go of the hatred and resentment. If you look deeply enough, you might find that within that hatred is also hatred for yourself, so you must also *forgive you*. The responsibility for the action is not yours. You were a victim, but to move forward now, you must become the victor. One way to do this is by recognizing how far you have grown and reach out to others who are just starting their journey of recovery. So much strength and wisdom comes when we open ourselves up to others and offer them a helping hand.

# EXERCISE

### REMEMBER TO
## VISUALIZE WHITE LIGHT

### -Putting on the Head of the Perpetrator-

Imagine that you have the ability to enter the thoughts of your perpetrator. I know that this may sound frightening, but it can also create a powerful release.

Now that you are in their head, I want you to reach back in their mind to their first memory. Look through their eyes at this first memory. Were they an infant? Were they receiving love and affection? Is the memory painful?

Keep moving forward in their memories and feel their feelings. What was their life like? What created the person that hurt you?

No one is born evil. Something changes us. Find that something and you may more easily also find the humanity, that God spark, that exists within all of us. At that point, it will be much easier to forgive this flawed human being and stop looking at them as powerful and evil and start seeing them for what they are: scared, unhappy, and deeply scarred.

# MEDITATION

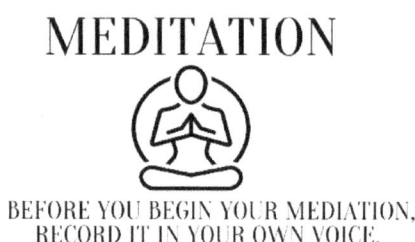

### BEFORE YOU BEGIN YOUR MEDIATION, RECORD IT IN YOUR OWN VOICE.

### -Release Childhood Pain-

Find a picture of yourself as a child. Sit comfortably in a quiet room where you will not be disturbed for at least 20 minutes. Begin to stare at the picture. What do you feel? Do you relate to this child? Do you like them? Are they cute, loveable, worthy? Analyze your feelings. Now close your eyes and allow your mind to go to the first memory you have of being this child. If you cannot retrieve a memory, make one up. It doesn't need to be real to work. Is the memory pleasant? Sad? Happy? Begin to feel what the child is feeling. What does the child need: appreciation, love, hope, support? See your adult-self entering this memory. If the child needs love, hold them, love them, and nurture them. If the child is frightened, tell the child you are here with them and that you will never leave, that all they need to do is call to you. Provide what they need. Allow yourself to feel the memory change, become whole, complete, then come back. If you don't feel cleansed, repeat this exercise until you do.

In no way am I saying that your pain is not real or that you deserve to have it, but I am saying that you don't need to keep feeling it. I am also aware that it may take much more than meditating or affirming. You might need professional help. Many of my clients go to both a counselor and me for help. We both work on the same issues, but offer different viewpoints and different tools. Set yourself free.

## QUESTIONS FOR FURTHER REFLECTION

**Review your significant childhood experiences. How have they shaped your life?**

Joan L. Scibienski

**Talk with a friend or relative about what they remember of their childhood. How does listening to their story help you to empathize? How does it help you understand your past better?**

**Ask one or both of your parents about what they remember of their childhood. Does listening to them help you understand them better? How?**

# LESSON 7
## WORKING WITH ENERGY PART 1
## HEALING

Spiritual Energy is what is within every living thing. It is the Universal Life Force and is considered to be a manifestation of pure love, that which is the essence of the Source or God and connects our ego to our soul. Many religions base their beliefs on this concept—that each person is connected to this spiritual energy. Through this connection to Divine loving energy—the Source—we are connected to everything and everyone.

It is with this energy, not your personal energy, that you can help to transform people, situations, and the planet. This is done through healing, enlightenment, and raising your vibration from fear to empowerment.

When studying metaphysics, you will find many different types of spiritual energy. Different cultures have assigned different names. There are four descriptions of spiritual energy that you will see most often:

**Prana** (Hindu): In its simplest English translation, prana means "breath" in Sanskrit but is more properly considered as life force energy . It is the energy that exists in all things, even human thoughts. This life-force energy survives death and can return through reincarnation.

**Chi** (Chinese): Is considered to be the energy current that runs through our bodies, containing both female (yin) and male (yang) energies. Working with Chi energy is an ancient art and is used today by doctors of integrative medicine and acupuncturists as a way to bring the body into balance, restoring the body to its natural, healthy state—to achieve a state of Zen. This is done by opening and balancing the energy vortexes in the body, or chakras.

The concept of **Divine Love** reoccurs within many different faiths like Christianity and Judaism. This spiritual energy is believed to be coming from God's divine love. This love is believed to be pure and cannot be corrupted. It is eternal and constant. This type of energy is most often activated through prayer.

**Mother Earth** energy is most often used by Native Americans, Wiccans, and Pagans. It is based on the belief that the earth and all creatures are sacred and filled with the divine energy of the Great Spirit. Mother Earth is considered to be a living entity and her energy can be used for healing and other things.

## Vibration and Vibrational Frequency

Because we are energy, we vibrate. We know from physics that even those things that appear to us to be solid are actually created by an underlying vibration. Our vibrations influence our mental states. They also influence our ability to manifest our desires.

When you want to attract something into your life, you must align with the frequency of its vibration. For example, if you are seeking love, you must believe in love and demonstrate it by being loving. The happier and more fulfilled your life feels, the higher your vibration. Gratitude is a wonderful way to increase your frequency. As you begin to live your life in the frequency of joy, your life becomes more joyous.

Mindfulness, meditation, and thinking through dilemmas rather than reacting, are ways to work on raising your vibration. Fill your home with beauty, sunshine, laughter, music, dance, meditation—all these expand the vibrations around you and thus help you to be conscious of where you are vibrating and help you learn to calibrate yourself to where you want to be. Be careful of surrounding yourself with negative people or situations as they will have the opposite effect.

## Distance Healing or Remote Healing

There are many different healing techniques, but one of the easiest is distance healing. Because everything is energy, time and place mean nothing. The key to healing is your intent and the understanding that you are much more than just your physical body. The basic premise of distance healing is that human beings are more than just their physical bodies; rather, each person also has an energy body comprised of their aura, chakras, and meridians—energy paths that flow within the body.

## How Distant Healing Works

Just like our physical body needs to eat to sustain it, our energy body takes in energy through the aura, which is distributed to the chakras and then distributed throughout the body by way of the meridians. And as mentioned, energy vibrates. This vibration can occur at different speeds or frequencies. It is possible to sense this pulsing, vibrating energy field. This field can be sensed or even felt through touch, for example.

## The Procedure

Before you can begin distance healing, find a quiet space where you can relax and think clearly. Begin by sitting or lying down in a comfortable position. Take a few deep breaths, and then ground and center yourself. *To center yourself*, first concentrate on your breathing. Breathe deeply, using your diaphragm to draw air all the way down into your lungs. Relax any muscles that feel tense by clenching them and then releasing them. Locate your "physical center of gravity" which, in centering, is visualized as being about two inches below your navel. Become familiar with where your center is and remember what it feels like. You'll probably find that you feel grounded and stabilized by focusing your mind on this part of your body.

As you breathe, picture in your imagination the energy moving through your body. See it moving from your feet to the top of your head. See the energy moving in one direction as you inhale, and then reverse the direction of the energy flow as you exhale.

Continue this visualization along with the breathing as you now bring your hands together, holding them in such a way as to form a small cup. Imagine the energy traveling to your cupped hands as you exhale. Picture the person or persons you are trying to heal and imagine that you are holding them in your hands. Or, if you are good at visualizing, visualize the person if you know them, or the form of a person if you do not, as you focus your attention on their name. Allow yourself to feel their energy. If you have trouble doing that, just keep focusing love, light, and healing on their name. Feel a tingling sensation or a warmth entering your body through your crown chakra, the top of your head, and believe that this is Divine Healing energy. Fill the other person with this energy. See them or feel them accepting this energy and see them or feel them well, happy, and complete. Imagine peace and love flowing into the hearts of those who are suffering, so that they may not only be healed physically, but mentally as well. Feel this as deeply as you can. Avoid doubt or negative energy or focusing on what is wrong.

Before you end your meditation, ask God—or whichever higher power you believe in—to bless those in need and bring peace to their lives. Take a deep breath before ending your healing session.

## Some Cautions

**Not everyone wants to be healed**. Some people receive benefit from being ill, like attention and love. They may not be conscious of this. But if this is their mindset, they will not receive or benefit from the healing. Please know that you did nothing wrong.

**Do not take in whatever illness is affecting the person**. Always remember to shield yourself, surrounding yourself in God's White Light of Protection, before beginning any remote or in-person healing. This is especially critical when you are in close proximity to the person you are focusing on. Don't allow yourself to focus on another's pain because then you will take it in yourself and actually drain yourself attempting to send them healing. You are not sending them healing but sending your own empathy.

**Do not send your own energy**. This caution raises an recent opportunity for me to learn. In our culture, it is a very common practice to hear someone say or write, "sending you thoughts and prayers." People with a more metaphysical approach often "send people energy." Regardless of the perspective you take, it is a beautiful thing to recognize our connections and ability to support each other.

But it is important to recognize that this practice needs to be done in a specific way to ensure that no harm is done to the sender. I recently realized that my good intentions to help others may have inadvertently been draining me. Quite often in my meditations, journaling, or just daily thoughts, I would think of a person and imagine good things for them. I was not mindful of a specific process for this, just that I was "sending energy" for them to use for their highest good.

Though my intention was good, my technique needed some improvement! For the last several decades, I have channeled a collective consciousness that calls themselves Equinoxx. (For more information on my channeling work: www.channelingeq.com) These First Friday channelings are open to the public and during the channelings, a Message for the World is shared, several general questions are asked, and then those in attendance are allowed to ask personal questions. The question of "giving energy" to others was addressed specifically in a recent channeling. The answer was as follows:

> "The way that we think is best is to begin to visualize the person and if you do not have a specific person in mind, or you have never seen the person, then all you need to do is see a general outline of a male or a female and then see them surrounded by God's energy, by God's beautious energetic light, and see it being absorbed into that body and see it radiating off and see the person laughing and jumping and just feeling marvelous. And then say, 'And so it is,' and release it. Release the picture. That's not your energy—you are giving them Universal God energy."

# EXERCISE

### REMEMBER TO VISUALIZE WHITE LIGHT

## Healing the Earth

The healing exercise described above can be done with the planet as well as humans and animals. Just visualize Earth and send her love and light. See her, and everything on her, healthy and working together for the benefit of all.

# EXERCISE

## REMEMBER TO
## VISUALIZE WHITE LIGHT

### Healing A Stranger

Ask a friend to give you the name of someone you do not know that has an illness. All they need to tell you is the full name and perhaps the age.

Go to a place you will not be disturbed, protect yourself with the White Light, get comfortable, and close your eyes. Practice some deep breathing for at least 3 repetitions focusing entirely on your breath. Now let your breath return to a normal, keeping it at a slow gentle rhythm as you focus on the person's name. Do you get a picture of the person in your mind? Do you feel anything different in your body or mind? Do you sense anything? Do you hear anything?

Write down anything you get, no matter how strange.

Ask your friend to check with this person and see if anything you perceived makes sense to them. Write about these findings here:

How did you feel while doing this exercise?

Did you try to censor any information? Why? What?

How did you receive the information? Through a feeling, a sense, something you saw, etc.

# LESSON 8
## WORKING WITH ENERGY PART 2
## AURAS

**What are Auras?** Before we can answer that question we need to review an important point: we are all energy housed in a physical body. This energy, however, cannot be entirely contained within our physical body and extends outward, usually about three feet. But an aura can also be much bigger or smaller depending on the disposition of the person, how safe they are feeling at the time, their mood, and whether the person has a traumatic past.

Some metaphysicians claim there are seven distinct layers to the aura and that each layer represents specific things. These layers are:

1. The **Etheric Field** which is the layer most closely tied to the physical body and can provide information about your health.

2. The **Emotional Field** which is about three inches from the body and provides information about your emotions.

3. The **Mental Field** which extends up to eight inches from the body and shows you mental processes, ideas, and thoughts.

4. The **Astral Layer** spreads out approximately one foot. It represents the bridge to the spiritual.

5. The **Etheric Template** extends two feet outward and is purported to contain the blueprint for the physical world. According to Phillip Rafferty, author of *Kinergetics Manual,* the blueprint is "a library, where records of all our experiences and memories, which relate to our Mental and Emotional Bodies, are placed, put in order, and retrieved by the Etheric Body. It holds the laws of physicality, for the emotional being and for the mental being." It helps us to navigate the physical plane and break through the illusions we live within.

6. The **Celestial Aura** can extend up to two-and-a-half feet and is connected to the spiritual realm and communication with that realm takes place here.

7. The **Causal or Ketheric Template** extends three feet or more, if well developed. This field is said to surround all the other fields and holds them together. It is also said to be the link to the Divine.

Auras can be felt, and with some training, seen. An aura is an ever-changing flow of energy emitted by any living thing. It can also be imprinted on objects and places. I am sure sometime in your past you have entered a building, and for no apparent reason, felt uncomfortable. If it was someone's house, perhaps you were feeling the hostile energy left over from an argument, the emotional energy left over by someone sick or dying, or the tumultuous energy left by a sudden change, such as a job loss. The house has been imprinted with the energy of the people who have lived there; it has been permeated by their auras.

Just as a house can accept your energy, an object that is treasured, worn often, that you are creating, or that something tragic happened around, will also be imbued with your energy. It is the basis of psychometry: the ability to pick up information through the energy left behind.

# REFLECTION

**Have you ever felt anything from a location?**

___
___
___
___
___
___
___
___
___
___
___

**Have you ever felt anything from an object?**

_____
_____
_____
_____
_____
_____
_____
_____
_____
_____
_____
_____

Many of us would answer no to the above questions. But what I've discovered through my many students is that it's not that they hadn't felt anything, they just hadn't noticed. Once they were instructed to pay attention to how they felt throughout the day and in different situations and locations, they became aware of how often they were receiving information. Awareness is key.

## Auras Also Have Color

Aura colors will change for various reasons, including your desire to change them. You can change the color by simply visualizing what color you want your aura to be. With some practice, this becomes easy.

Here are some general descriptions of what the colors mean and what affect the color may have both on the body and the personality.

**Red** – pertains to circulation and the heart. People with red auras are said to be physical, energetic, competitive, passionate, powerful, sexual, and highly charged individuals. They can be quick to anger and display violent tendencies or be filled with anxiety and nervousness. It is best to limit the use of this color. If this is your natural color, you can mitigate it by simply visualizing the color blue.

**Pink** – sensual, artistic, loving, and sensitive. It can appear when a new or revived relationship is in one's life.

**Orange** – reproductive organs and emotions. It can represent good health, vitality, and creativity. This person is usually productive, courageous, and out-going, but can also be a perfectionist, and due to the red in it, can create stress.

**Yellow** – pertains to the spleen and life energy and shows a generally happy, vibrant, optimistic, easy-going, and intelligent person. This color can also show awakening.

**Green** – pertains to the heart and lungs and usually shows good health. Green depicts a love of animals and nature as well as the ability to be a healer. It also indicates growth and balance and potential change.

**Blue** – associated with the thyroid, throat, and immune system. This color represents a sensitive, loving, caring, compassionate person who may also be empathic, intuitive, and often clairvoyant with natural qualities to be a healer, counselor, or therapist.

**Indigo** – pertains to the third eye (the area in the brain, at the brow and above the base of the nose, which allows us access to our inner guidance) and pituitary gland, and is the color of deep feeling, intuition, and sensitivity.

**Violet** – pertains to the crown chakra, pineal gland, and nervous system and is said to be intuitive, visionary, artistic, and psychic.

**Silver** – may mean money or spiritual awakening.

**Gold** – Divine protection, inner peace, wisdom, enlightenment, and spiritual guidance. Associated with an inspired, awakened person.

**Brown** – could indicate being grounded or greedy, insensitive, ill, self-absorbed, closed-minded, or resentful.

**Black** – illness, grief, unresolved anger, corruption, a severely damaged individual. They may be holding deep negativity, even psychosis, and be dangerous.

**White** – can indicate protection, truth, purity, and angelic qualities. This is usually the first color you will be able to see.

There are also variations on the above colors like lime-green, aqua, or tan for example, but the above list represents the colors you will usually see.

# EXERCISE

## REMEMBER TO
## VISUALIZE WHITE LIGHT

**What is your favorite color and why?**

_____
_____
_____
_____

**What is the color of most of the clothing you own?**

_____
_____
_____
_____

We are often drawn to the primary color in our aura. When you wear a color that compliments your aura, you will usually get compliments from others even though they do not know they are seeing your aura. When you wear colors that clash with your aura, people will comment that the color is unflattering even if they had complimented you previously on how good you looked in it. That is because our auras change. Your primary aura, the Etheric, usually does not. But the others do, depending on your health, mood, and your spiritual development.

**What do various colors feel like to you? Are they cool, warm, comfortable, uncomfortable?**

_____
_____
_____
_____
_____
_____
_____
_____
_____

This is another example of not paying attention. Most people have no idea how colors feel to them—they've never paid attention. Cut up swatches of felt material of different colors and sizes. Close your eyes and without knowing what color you are holding, feel what you are feeling. Open your eyes and look at the color. What are you feeling now? Some blind people feel color. That's how they can tell them apart.

## REMEMBER TO
# VISUALIZE WHITE LIGHT

### Find Your Aura

- ❖ Protect yourself, then ground and center yourself. As explained earlier, *to center yourself*, first concentrate on your breathing; breathe deeply, using your diaphragm to draw air all the way down into your lungs. Relax any muscles that feel tense by clenching them and then releasing them. Locate your "physical center of gravity" which, in centering, is visualized as being about two inches below your navel. Become familiar with where your center is and remember what it feels like. You'll probably find that you feel grounded and stabilized by focusing your mind on this part of your body.

- ❖ Imagine all the energy in your body flowing into your center like a sun burning there. Focus all your attention on this energy and relax. Now visualize a silver cord leave your body from the base of your spine and descend deeply into the earth. You are now grounded and centered.

- ❖ Rub your hands briskly together then spread them approximately 12 to 15 inches apart. Bring them together very slowly until you feel a "spongey" resistance. When you contact this resistance, you are feeling your own aura.

*For the rest of the exercises you will need another person.*

# EXERCISE

### REMEMBER TO
## VISUALIZE WHITE LIGHT

### Investigating Another's Aura

- ❖ Have your friend, the "subject," sit facing you. If they are taller than you, seat them in a chair in the center of the room so that you can walk around them. Rub your hands together again and then place your hands as far above the subject's head as you can reach. Feel for that same resistance you felt between your own hands. Once you have felt the resistance, you are now inside their aura.

- ❖ Begin to slowly bring your hands around their body feeling for areas that feel either hot or cold, that are vibrating, or have no feeling or vibration at all. Note the areas that are feeling different to you and ask your subject if they've been having problems in those areas or if they had any past injury in that particular area. Sometimes they will say they haven't noticed anything. Don't be disheartened as whatever you are feeling may not have manifested as a problem yet. When the subject gives you positive feedback, pay attention to what they say. Note what they say was wrong or what problem they had with the area in the past, so that next time you encounter this feeling on another subject, you can ascertain that perhaps it is the same condition.

# EXERCISE

### REMEMBER TO
## VISUALIZE WHITE LIGHT

### Predict the Condition

After you have become proficient at feeling a person's energy, try doing the previous exercise and see if you can figure out what the condition is *before the subject tells you*. If you are an empath, you might actually feel the pain. Do not take it on! Release it as soon as the session is over.

# EXERCISE

### REMEMBER TO
## VISUALIZE WHITE LIGHT

### Healing

- ❖ If you choose to attempt a healing, first get permission from the subject and then put your non-dominant hand in the air, palm facing upward.

- ❖ Fill your mind with the desire and intent to be an instrument of healing. Begin to feel God's healing energy enter that hand. (You might feel your hand or your entire body grow very warm.) Then channel that energy through your body to your dominant hand and send the energy into the spot that needs healing. You can do this by actually touching the body or hovering over it with your hand.

- ❖ **Shake your hands in the air when you are through with each session, asking the Universe and your guides to take away the energy and illnesses of the other person and then go wash your hands with soap and water.**

# EXERCISE

### REMEMBER TO
## VISUALIZE WHITE LIGHT

### Seeing Colors

Seeing auras is actually quite easy if you give yourself permission. Seeing colors is slightly harder, but all it takes is a little practice.

- ❖ Place a subject against a white or very pale colored background. Seat yourself several feet away, looking up at the subject. When your eyes are at a slight 45-degree-angle, your brain enters a slightly more relaxed brainwave state. This is only necessary until you become used to seeing auras.

- Stare at a spot approximately 10 inches above the subject's head and let your eyes become unfocused. Keep staring as long as you can without blinking. Eventually you will notice a white light surrounding the body. Some people's auras extend way out from their bodies, other people keep theirs very close. Auras can have bulges, spikes, holes, even other people or objects within them. Like seeing colors, it may take practice to recognize some of these things.

- As you continue staring, allow your eyes to travel down the body. See if you see any changes, especially other colors. All of this takes practice. Don't give up.

# EXERCISE
### REMEMBER TO
## VISUALIZE WHITE LIGHT

### Changing the Colors

All of us have a colored aura, but as mentioned earlier, that color can change. Colors can change due to mood, health, marriage, pregnancy, motherhood or fatherhood, or our environment. You can also change the color of your aura by thinking about an emotion or scene associated with a color; thinking of the sky or ocean may invoke a blue. Feeling happy or the sun on your skin may invoke yellow. Thoughts of purity or love can change the aura to white. This can be a very useful ability. For instance, imagine if you wanted to make a good impression on someone. Turning your aura yellow can help the person feel comfortable with you because they will perceive you as a happy, friendly, nice person.

# MEDITATION

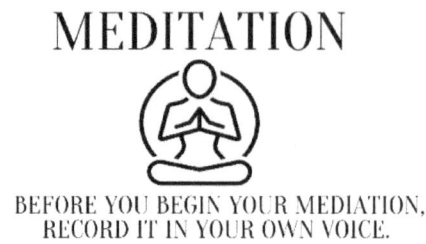

BEFORE YOU BEGIN YOUR MEDIATION,
RECORD IT IN YOUR OWN VOICE.

## Healing with Color

Close your eyes and visualize sitting on a beach. The intense, blue sky is being reflected by the water so that except for the whitecaps, the sea and sky are an intense shade of blue. The entire environment is calm, pristine. As you sit staring out at this expanse of blue, feel yourself calm. As the waves break around you, as they go in-and-out, in-and-out, feel yourself getting more and more relaxed, going deeper and deeper into this state of calm, this deep, calming, intense blue. Breathe in the color blue. Feel your energy blending with the energy of the sea and the sky, becoming calm, becoming blue. Merge your energy—become the color blue. Be the calm. Be the peace. Be blue. Whenever you want to be calm, all you need to do is visualize the color blue, the color that is the sea and the sky, and you will calm. From now on, the color blue will calm you. From now on, visualizing the sea or the sky will calm you. It is that easy.

Open your eyes but retain this calm state. You are one with the sea and the sky. You are one with the color blue. You are calm. So it is and you let it be.

We feel other people's auras even when we don't realize it. Have you ever been somewhere that people are standing very close to you? Often, we react poorly to someone in "our personal space"—which is really just another name for aura. To test this, I have two students who do not know each other very well begin to walk toward each other one step at a time. With each step I ask them to tell me how they are feeling. When they get within a foot or two of each other they usually confess they are feeling uncomfortable. Many of us have problems being touched or hugged by someone we don't really know well because our auras are merging, and if you are empathic it is worse because within someone's aura you can pick up information about them, including feeling their physical and emotional pain. If you are shielded this is less likely, even with close contact.

# QUESTIONS FOR FURTHER REFLECTION

**How do you feel when someone is too close to you?**

**What can you learn by observing the aura of someone you like? Someone you don't like? Someone you are attracted to?**

# LESSON 9

## WORKING WITH ENERGY PART 3
## CHAKRAS

**Chakras are the energy centers** in our bodies. They are like the vortices on land where people go to feel energy. In us, they are where energy flows into and out of our physical body to our non-physical selves and the Universe.

The word chakra is a Sanskrit word meaning wheel or disk. There are seven main chakras. They align along the spine, starting from the base (right above the tailbone) to the crown of the head. The chakras are like a swirling wheel of energy where matter and consciousness meet. This invisible energy, called Prana, is vital life-force energy. It keeps us vibrant, healthy, and alive.

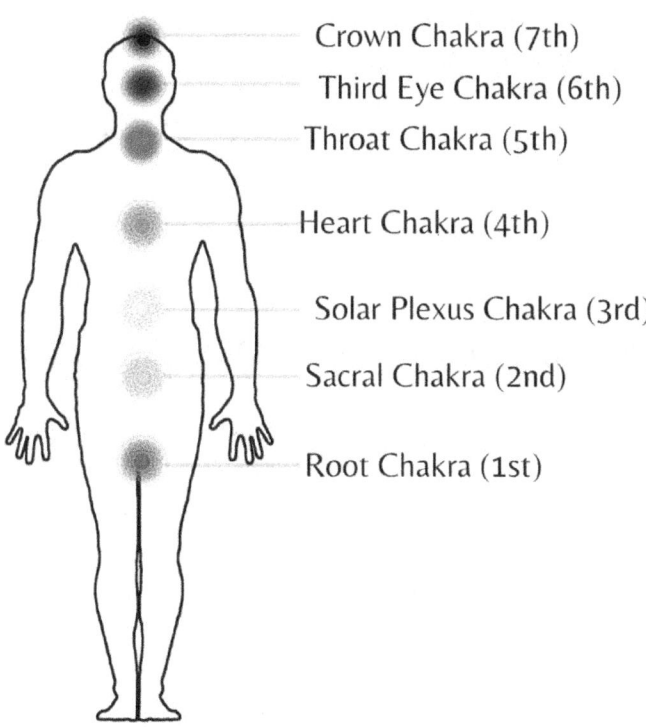

Crown Chakra (7th)
Third Eye Chakra (6th)
Throat Chakra (5th)
Heart Chakra (4th)
Solar Plexus Chakra (3rd)
Sacral Chakra (2nd)
Root Chakra (1st)

These moving wheels of energy are connected to the nerve centers in the body. Within the seven main chakras are bundles of nerves and organs as well as our psychological, emotional, and spiritual states of being. Since the wheels are always moving, it's essential that our seven main chakras stay open, aligned, and fluid. If there is a blockage, energy cannot flow and will eventually create disease and problems within your life-force.

## The Chakras that Correspond with the Physical Realm

Starting at the base of the spine, the first three chakras are chakras of matter. They are more physical in nature.

**The first chakra** is called the Muladhara or root chakra and is concerned with stability, security, and our basic needs. It encompasses the first three vertebrae, the bladder, and the colon. When this chakra is open, we feel safe and fearless. When it is closed, we are insecure, fearful, and miserly. It is associated with childhood and family matters.

**The second chakra** is called the Svadhisthana or sacral chakra. It is the seat of creativity and sexuality. It is located above the pubic bone and below the navel. It is responsible for our creative expression. It is blocked when sexual abuse or sexual guilt is present, thus blocking our creativity.

**The third chakra** is the Manipura or solar plexus chakra. It is the area from the navel to the breastbone. The third chakra is our source of personal power. When closed, you often have a feeling of helplessness.

## The Connection Between Matter and Spirit:

**The fourth chakra** is located at the heart center and is called Anahata or heart chakra. It is at the middle of the seven chakras and unites the lower chakras of matter and the upper chakras of spirit. The fourth is also spiritual but serves as a bridge between our body, mind, emotions, and spirit. The heart chakra is our source of love and connection. When closed, you may feel unloved, unlovable, and be unable to return love.

When we work through our physical chakras, the first three, we can open the spiritual chakras more fully and begin to use more of our power and unite more completely with the Universe.

## The Chakras of Spirit

**The fifth chakra** is called the Vishuddha chakra or the throat chakra. This is our source of verbal expression and the ability to speak our highest truth. The fifth chakra includes the neck, thyroid and parathyroid glands, jaw, mouth, and tongue. When closed, you may have problems with communication, being heard or understood, or understanding others.

**The sixth chakra** is called the Ajna chakra or the third eye chakra and is located between the eyebrows. Ajna is our center of intuition and focus and allows us to see the big picture. When closed, you may be closed-minded, skeptical, and lack intuition.

**The seventh chakra** is the Sahaswara chakra or the Thousand Petal Lotus chakra which is located at the crown of the head and is often referred to as the crown chakra. This is the chakra of enlightenment and spiritual connection to our higher selves, others, and ultimately, to the Divine. It is located at the crown of the head.

## Aligning the Chakras

Awareness of which of your chakras are out of balance is key to aligning them. Our bodies are in constant flux between balance and imbalance. Unless you have an apparent problem in one area of the body, imbalances can be difficult to detect. Learn to have an awareness of what is happening in your body, what stresses you are under, how much of your past is affecting your present, so that you can recognize which chakras may be out of balance and why. Observe your body and mind and start to learn its signals and clues.

For example, frequent constipation can indicate a blockage in the first chakra. A recurring sore throat leaves clues to a blocked fifth chakra. Frequent headaches around the area of the forehead may mean your sixth chakra is blocked.

The first step to unblocking chakras may be to ascertain what these chakras indicate. In the example of the blocked first chakra, what emotional pain are you holding in and not dealing with? The blocked fifth chakra may indicate that you are afraid to take a stand, to speak your truth, while the headaches may be telling you that you are not seeing the larger picture in a fair and impartial way.

# Exercise 1: Self Reflection

**Where are you experiencing pain in your body and what chakra corresponds with the area?**

**Can you identify any emotional or spiritual reasons for your pain?**

**How might these situations from your past be blocking your chakras, keeping you stuck?**

**What steps can you take to let go of these past hurts?**

# MEDITATION

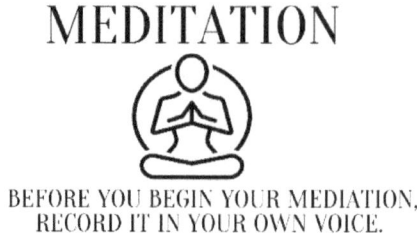

BEFORE YOU BEGIN YOUR MEDIATION, RECORD IT IN YOUR OWN VOICE.

## Exercise 2: Meditation to Examine Physical Pain

Make yourself comfortable and begin breathing slowly through your nose and exhaling slowly through your mouth. Focus your entire attention on your breathing. Breathe like this for 5 complete breaths. Continue breathing in this way, but now, with each inhalation of breath, allow yourself to relax. Hear and see the word *relax* in your mind. Now, when you exhale, feel your body growing warm and relaxing. Do the breathing exercise until you are feeling completely relaxed.

Let yourself begin to feel your body. Look for any areas that are feeling painful, ill, or out of balance. Feel the energy in all the parts of your body starting with your head, then your face and everything on your face, your neck, shoulders—keep going throughout your body. When you come across an area that does not feel quite right, ask it what it needs. **Listen**. If you truly listen and believe, you will hear what is wrong and what you need to do to fix this area. Do what is described. It may be a change of diet, a massage or adjustment, or healing an old emotional experience.

*Do this exercise every day until your body comes into balance.*

**What did your body tell you?**

___
___
___
___
___
___
___
___
___
___
___
___
___
___

## What is your plan?

## *One week later* – journal your results:

# MEDITATION

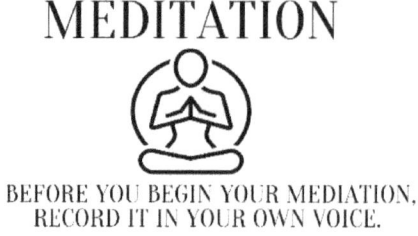

BEFORE YOU BEGIN YOUR MEDIATION,
RECORD IT IN YOUR OWN VOICE.

## Exercise 3: Meditation to Receive Information

Let yourself completely relax and begin to breathe like you did in the previous meditation. When you are finally very relaxed, begin to count down from 10 to one very slowly, reminding yourself that you can relax even deeper; 10 times deeper or 100 times deeper, just breathe and relax. When you get to the number five, reinforce that when you reach the number one you will be completely and utterly relaxed and that any sounds you hear will only send you more deeply into relaxation. When you reach the number one, feel yourself as more relaxed than you've ever been before and allow yourself to luxuriate in that feeling.

Now, let your consciousness begin to roam the areas of your chakras starting at the root chakra. Pay attention to the area at the base of your spine. Can you feel a tingling of energy or a vibration? What direction is it spinning?

Now move up to the second chakra right below your belly button. Again, see if you can sense any energy and if so, what way is it moving?

Continue your way slowly up your body until you have reached the crown chakra, looking for any feeling of energy and ascertaining if it is moving, and if so, which direction.

**What did you feel?**

___
___
___
___
___
___
___
___

## Which chakras were open?

## Which were closed?

**Were each of the chakras spinning the same direction? Write down which chakra and the direction it was moving: clockwise, counter-clockwise.**

**Root:**

**Sacral:**

**Solar Plexus:**

**Heart:**

**Throat:**

**Third Eye:**

**Crown:**

_____
_____
_____
_____

*Continuing with the mediation...*

Now, begin to visualize each chakra, starting at the base and moving up very slowly. Visualize the chakras as a flower and gently see it going from a bud to a fully-blooming flower that is vibrant, healthy, and filled with energy. Send your conscious energy to each of these chakras and ascertain if there is a need to fix anything.

Count yourself back by telling yourself that you will count from one to five and when you reach the number five you will feel wonderful; healthy, happy, and feeling much better than before. When you are fully back in the present, write down what the experience was like and what you learned.

_____
_____
_____
_____
_____
_____
_____
_____
_____
_____
_____
_____
_____
_____
_____
_____
_____
_____

Often you can feel if a chakra is open, especially the third eye. Your forehead will tingle and you might feel uncomfortable having anything over it, or on the contrary, you might feel better when it is covered.

## Exercise 4: Using a Pendulum to Check Chakras

This exercise requires two people. Have a friend lie on their stomach on the floor. Put your pendulum in your dominant hand and suspend it approximately six inches above the root chakra. Hold it steady and wait a full minute. Record any movement and, if it spins, the direction. Move to the next chakra and repeat. Continue all the way to the crown, recording what the pendulum does.

**Root:**

_____
_____
_____
_____

**Sacral:**

_____
_____
_____
_____

**Solar Plexus:**

_____
_____
_____
_____

**Heart:**

_____
_____
_____
_____

**Throat:**

_____
_____
_____
_____

**Third Eye:**

_____
_____
_____
_____

**Crown:**

_____
_____
_____
_____

## Exercise 5: Opening and Balancing

*For this exercise, it is best to have at least four people and the subject.*

- Have the subject lie on their stomach on the floor. Do exactly what you did in Exercise 4 to check the chakras and see which are open and which are closed. Have one person seated at the feet of the subject, the other at the head. Seat yourself at the solar plexus chakra of the subject with the fourth person across from you.

- Put your hands above the throat and solar plexus chakras. The person across from you should place their hands above the heart and base chakras. The person at the head places one hand above the third eye and one at the crown chakra. The person at the feet puts their hands facing but not touching the souls of the subject's bare feet.

- Direct the person at the head to begin to build their energy and fill the crown chakra by visualizing white light of healing, balancing energy. Ask the subject if they are feeling the warmth or vibration of the energy. When he or she reports they are feeling it, tell the subject to feel the energy building in their crown chakra as the attendants, you and the other three people, send energy to the crown chakra. To send energy, focus on feeling energy and warmth entering your body, fill your body with energy, then visualize that energy going from your hands or third eye, directly to the subject.

- When the energy is feeling intense, tell the subject to send the energy that's in the crown chakra down their body, like flushing the energy down a toilet. The subject should visualize and feel the energy careening down their body. You and the attendant across from you should be able to feel the energy going through the chakras. The person at the feet should feel a rush of energy come from the feet and into their hands if it worked.

- Check the chakras again with a pendulum to determine if all the chakras are now open and in balance, spinning in the same direction. If not, repeat the procedure again. If the chakras are open and balanced, have the subject sit up slowly. They should be feeling great, but can be slightly dizzy from the intense intake of energy. The attendants should wash their hands.

**Could you feel or see the energy as it went through the subject's body?**

**Be the subject and write what this experience felt like and how you felt afterward:**

If the balancing is done effectively, you should at first feel light headed, then energized. Some people become a bit giddy. If healing energy is sent at the same time, those areas will either feel healed or better than they did before the balancing was done.

# LESSON 10
## PSYCHOMETRY

**Psychometry is a psychic ability** in which a person can sense or "read" the history of an object, place, or person by touching that object. The reason this is possible is because all matter, everything in the Universe, is energy. When your energy is placed on an object—a piece of jewelry you wear often, for instance—some of that energy remains and can be felt from the object. The same is true of places, especially those that hold a heavy charge like a battlefield or Pearl Harbor, or even a home where a lot of happiness or sadness has permeated the walls and floors.

The trick to psychometry is to trust what you get, whether it is a feeling, a sense of something, a sound, smell, or taste. You may even visualize something. This takes practice. It is likely that your left brain, the logical side, will try to put an explanatory spin on any information you may receive from the object. For example, let's say you are holding a woman's ring. The left side of your brain will tell you that the object belongs or belonged to a woman. If the setting looks antique, you might conclude that it is old and has been in a family for a while, so it must be a treasured keepsake. But in truth it is also possible that the ring holds pain and disappointment as it is owned by a man who bought it just recently to give to a girl he liked, but when he tried to give it to her, she rebuffed him, causing a lot of hurt and sorrow.

## EXERCISE

### REMEMBER TO VISUALIZE WHITE LIGHT

**Object Psychometry**

It is impossible to get accurate psychic information by using logic. Consequently, I suggest that as you are practicing, have someone put a small object into your hand without you looking at it. Once it is in your palm, close your fingers and feel the shape and texture of the object. Then, close your eyes and allow yourself to sense the object—*feel it*. Do you sense a feeling of happiness, sadness, expectation, discomfort? Do you see anything: colors, objects, a scene? Do you smell or taste anything? How does your body feel? Any new aches, pains or physical sensations? Just relax and say *anything* that comes to mind, no matter how ridiculous you might think it is. Let go of that logical, left-side of your brain. Release the creative and intuitive right-side.

# EXERCISE
### REMEMBER TO
## VISUALIZE WHITE LIGHT

## Place Psychometry

Place psychometry works similarly to object psychometry. Years ago, when I sold real estate, I was often surprised how frequently people would walk into a house and say, "It just doesn't feel right" or "Something feels off." These weren't even people that considered themselves intuitive. When I would go back and research the properties I would often find divorce, violence, or sickness connected with the house.

If you go to a place that is known for having had a catastrophe, focus on what you are feeling. Often people feel like crying. They rationalize it's because something bad happened there, but I've seen it happen even when the person doesn't know where they are. When I was walking through an ancient Roman bath in Bath, England, I came upon an altar to a goddess. Not thinking, I put my hand on it to see what I could feel. Immediately, I felt terror. I felt like I needed to throw up. Later, after researching this goddess, I discovered it was reported that children were sacrificed as an offering to her on that very altar.

Becoming proficient in psychometry takes a lot of practice. *Here are some suggestions:*

> ❖ Have someone put pictures in opaque envelopes. The more these pictures mean to the person, the more intense the subject matter, or the more vibrant the colors, the better. Now, hold the envelope in your hand and focus your attention on it for a minute or two. Feel

your feelings, senses, and whatever else you get. If you get nothing, move to the next envelope until you have gone through the lot. Notice how often you went "left-brain" instead of just letting the sensations flow.

- ❖ Have a friend gather together objects from other people, finding out the history of the objects, then have that person hand the objects to you one at a time while you again concentrate on what you are getting.

- ❖ Always use protection! Do not judge your ability. Do not compare yourself to anyone else. We all start at different places and all have different abilities. Keep practicing.

# MEDITATION

BEFORE YOU BEGIN YOUR MEDIATION, RECORD IT IN YOUR OWN VOICE.

## Feel Joyful Energy

Go to a place known for joyous events: a local park or entertainment center. Surround yourself with protection. Sit quietly and allow yourself to relax. Breathe deeply and begin your countdown from ten to one, relaxing your body and your mind. When you reach the number one, allow yourself to feel the energy that surrounds you. Can you feel the laughter and the joy? If you feel capable of doing it, begin to walk around. Are there areas that draw your attention, that seem to pull you toward them or push you away? Try to notice the subtle energies that surround you.

## QUESTIONS FOR FURTHER REFLECTION

Do you recall being somewhere new but having a sensation of familiarity or even receiving information?

_____
_____
_____
_____
_____
_____
_____
_____
_____
_____
_____
_____
_____
_____
_____
_____
_____
_____
_____
_____

I have problems with antiques and second-hand stores. Often I pick up too much when I enter them. Places that have a lot of old things in them are great places to practice your shielding and protections.

Be aware of places that might create a reaction. I personally would never go to a concentration camp, Pearl Harbor, or Hiroshima. I'm afraid that the horrific energy that still permeates these places would overwhelm me even with my shields. I choose not to test that belief.

# LESSON 11

## CLAIRVOYANCE

**The term clairvoyance** (French for "clear vision") refers to the ability to gain information about an object, person, location or physical event through means other than the five accepted human senses. It is often called extrasensory perception (ESP). For some, clairvoyance appears innate. For most people, it can be redeveloped through various psychic exercises, meditation, and practice.

Nearly everyone experiences ESP at some time in their lives. There have been a number of accounts of clairvoyance happening spontaneously among the general population. For example, many people report seeing a loved one who has recently died before they learned by other means that they were deceased, or a mother knows something has happened to one of her children, or someone decides not to fly on a certain airline and later finds out there was an accident or delay on that flight. These are spontaneous clairvoyant events.

Often people receive clairvoyant dreams. This is one reason to be sure to record all your dreams. Clairvoyant dreams may be different from ordinary dreams as they may appear clearer and as though you are watching the event instead of participating in it. However, this is not always the case as the following example from my own life illustrates.

I dreamed that I was sitting on my car with my boyfriend at the time at a remote spot in Indiana. Teenagers called it "The Haunted Bridge." We were talking and listening to music on the car radio when a news broadcast broke into the music announcing that everyone in this specific county needed to be cautious because wolves were prowling the area killing people. Frightened, I turned to my boyfriend to suggest we leave, but when I turned to talk with him he had transformed into a werewolf! He then proceeded to tear my throat out and kill me. At this point, I immediately woke from the dream.

No matter how hard I tried to interpret the dream, I could see nothing in my life that it could pertain to. My boyfriend, Joe, was a sweet, gentle boy and there were no wolves in the area. I chalked it up to just another nightmare and went on with my normal life.

Two years later, Joe and I were married. On his 21st birthday I bought him a bottle of champagne to celebrate. Perhaps it was a genetic or allergic reaction, but it brought out the beast in him. He became a violent alcoholic who eventually attempted to murder me.

Years later, I came across my old dream journal and reread the dream. Although all this happened somewhere around five years after the dream, I realized the dream had foretold it. It had been a clairvoyant dream.

You can begin to finely tune this ability with practice. All you need to do is begin to pay attention, while both awake and asleep, to what you feel and see, especially those feelings or senses that cannot otherwise be explained by usual means. Don't disregard your hunches as they could someday save your life.

## Exercise 1: Zener Cards

These cards are used in most psychic testing, especially when looking for clairvoyance. They consist of a deck made up of five simple symbols. The five different Zener Cards are: a circle, a plus sign, three vertical wavy lines (or "waves"), a square, and a five-pointed star. There are 25 cards in a pack, five of each design.

During the test, the person conducting the test (the experimenter) picks up a card in a shuffled pack, observes the symbol on the card, and asks the testee to tell him or her what the symbol on the card is and then records the answer. The experimenter continues until all the cards in the pack have been tested. Make sure to shuffle well.

If there is psychic ability, the success ratio is expected to approach 20% (1 hit per 5 trials) as the number of trials increases. It is also relevant to note if the testee is doing much poorer than chance (less than 10%) as this too, can show ability. In this case, the person being tested is using their abilities to sabotage the results.

## QUESTIONS FOR FURTHER REFLECTION

**How did you feel while doing this exercise: interested, assured, fearful?**

**How often did you try to identify the card by being logical instead of just going with your first instinct? How could you prevent doing this in the future?**

## Exercise 2: Honing Your Skills to Find Lost Objects

In this exercise, you will begin to see how different objects are perceived by your inner knowing. Have a friend put five objects on a tray. Begin staring at the tray, attempting to memorize in detail all five objects. Do this for 10 seconds then have the tray removed. Now write down or draw as many objects as you remember, in as much detail as you can. When you get good at doing this with five objects, increase the number to ten. This exercise will help with both visualization and sensing.

## Exercise 3: Finding Lost Objects

Have someone hide five objects in a room. This exercise can be done in two ways: you may either be told in advance what the objects are or have them kept secret. If you are not told what the objects are, they should be things that would not naturally belong in the room.

Take a seat and put yourself in a relaxed, possibly meditative state. Allow your consciousness to sense what is different in the room. If you know what the objects are, you may concentrate on them. If not, sense what is unique in this room. Send out your consciousness much like you did in the exercises for remote viewing.

If you know one of the objects is a leather wallet, concentrate on the smell of leather, its feel, and what it may contain. Obviously, the same can be done with food.

Mentally ask questions and then listen for answers. Some examples might be: is it covered up? Is it under something or behind something? Is it in darkness or light?

# QUESTIONS FOR FURTHER REFLECTION

**Would it have been harder if the object was alive? How?**

_____
_____
_____
_____
_____
_____
_____
_____

## Exercise 4: Stop Lights

Plan a route to a location you do not normally drive. Before leaving, concentrate on the route and ask your inner knowing, "How many red lights will I have to stop for on my route?" You should receive a number. While driving, make sure you do not alter your speed by going faster or slower in order to skew the results. Count the red lights. How accurate were you?

## Exercise 5: Telephone

For an entire week whenever you receive a text or call, see if you can determine who is calling or texting you before you check the phone.

## QUESTIONS FOR FURTHER REFLECTION

**How often did you use logic instead of instinct? Why?**

**How do you feel about being able to predict the future?**

**What happens if you see something tragic? How would you deal with it?**

# LESSON 12

## DREAMS & HOW TO WORK WITH THEM

*"A dream which is not interpreted is like a letter which is not read."* ~The Talmud

**So much has been written about dreams,** but many people do not take them seriously. Many assume that dreams just happen when you sleep, with no conscious effort or control on your part. Dreams, however, are a gateway to understanding. They can help you to realize what is blocking your efforts, what internal work must be done so that you can move forward, or can actually be a communication with your guides, angels, or deceased loved ones. They can be prophetic, informational, or answer questions that you have been wondering about all day. You can use dreams to problem solve, make decisions, and examine a problem. What uses you put your dreams toward depends mainly on your imagination.

### Types of Dreams

There are many different types of dreams you will encounter once you begin keeping a journal and paying attention. Some of these you will be familiar with, others not so much. How you work with interpreting these dreams may be somewhat different because some will be obvious while others will require the use of a technique.

1. **Nightmare:** In nightmares you awaken frightened, often with a memory of what you have dreamt, which can linger for years. They often represent repressed memories. These memories are being shown to you so that you can take some action to alleviate the situation. Nightmares can also represent anger, fear, resentment or pain that you must release in some way. You are avoiding dealing with them, so your subconscious mind forces them out into the open. It can also show you a problem you are having with an authority figure.

2. **Shadow dreams:** These dreams reveal parts of ourselves that we do not want to recognize nor deal with. These shadow parts are creating problems in your life and come to the surface so that we can admit them and seek a solution.

3. **Recurring dream:** These are dreams that you have more than once. It can occur nightly for a length of time or reoccur at different times in our lives. They often represent things that we have not resolved, and the dream is an attempt to find the resolution.

4. **Creative and problem-solving dreams:** Have you ever been working on a problem or thinking deeply on a topic, only to have the answer come to you in a dream? That is a problem-solving dream. These dreams will show you possibilities that have eluded your waking mind.

5. **Precognitive:** These are dreams that foretell events in the future.

6. **Warning dreams:** They can be, or appear to be, precognitive but actually occur because you are noticing something in your environment that is alerting you to a problem you are not consciously aware of, like illness or accident. Maybe you are partially conscious that you are driving less cautiously, but you chose to ignore those thoughts. That evening you have a dream that you have a car accident.

7. **Lucid dream:** This is a dream in which you realize you are dreaming and you can interact with the dream. You can even change situations within the dream. You can be taught to use this dream state. Lucid dreaming is a complex topic that will be covered in the following lesson.

8. **Wish fulfillment:** For adults, these are often sexual dreams. For children, they indicate desires. In the dream you have the opportunity to experience something you would like to occur in your waking life.

9. **Communication dream:** These dreams can be a sentence or phrase. They carry a message from guides, angels, or deceased persons. Make sure you analyze and examine the message so that you get the full impact.

10. **Clearing dream:** These dreams are your mind attempting to rid itself of the day's events. Imagine that you have spent the day working on a proposal and that night you have a dream that you are in front of a group giving a presentation nude. That may be your mind attempting to sort through your fears about the presentation. The same is true if you've spent the day studying for a test and you dream that you are taking the test and you are unprepared.

11. **Big dream:** These are intense dreams, not necessarily nightmares, that stick with you for years. Even as the time goes on, the details remain sharp and vivid.

12. **Information dream:** In these dreams, no interpretation is needed; it is exactly as it appears. It may be like a message dream as it could be communication from the other side.

13. **Social dreams:** They are the mind dealing with events within our society. During war time they can be dreams of blood and death, for instance.

14. **Past life dreams:** Like the name implies, they are memories of past life. They will appear more vivid, clearer, and familiar. It will feel different than other types of dreams.

When you are interpreting your dreams it is important to understand that you can have dreams that fit in multiple categories. For instance, you can have a nightmare about a past life that is a warning and a communication.

Many of my clients have complained that they don't remember their dreams, or when they do, the dreams make no sense. Certainly, the language of dreams is quite different from the language of our everyday world. But like learning any foreign language, dream interpretation takes some knowledge, patience, and practice.

So, let me give you the key and some practical suggestions to help you begin to remember your dreams and to teach you how to apply them in your waking life.

## Remembering Your Dreams

For the initial stage of this training, make sure you go to bed early enough to relax and set the stage.

### Step 1: Exercise to Remember Your Dreams

- ❖ Next to your bed, place a writing implement, paper, and a light source that is easily reached. Prepare yourself for sleep in your usual way then lie back, close your eyes, and begin to breathe deeply and slowly—in through your nose and out your mouth. Focus your mind and concentrate completely on your breathing, allowing your body to relax. Let all thoughts that enter your mind just flow through as you focus on your breathing.

- ❖ After you feel that your body is relaxed, tell yourself that you will dream tonight, and at the dream's conclusion, you will be awakened and you will remember your dream. Allow your mind to be imprinted with this thought, vision, and desire. Focus on it. After a few seconds, allow your mind to imagine that you are floating—floating toward sleep. Feel your body relaxing even further and begin to get very sleepy. Allow your body and mind to drift naturally into sleep.

❖ When you are awakened, **do not** get up. If you get up the dream will be lost. Move as little as possible, turn on the light, and begin recording everything you can remember of the dream. Don't try to make sense of anything yet. Just write everything including colors, people, terrain, buildings, pets, words, including signs, dates, and random words. Include anything that is said or done and any impressions you had about the dream. Were you fearful, happy, sad, excited? What was your mood? Put as much detail as possible. Now, if it's appropriate, go back to sleep. If you awake again, do the same thing.

You might need to do this exercise several days in a row before you actually are awakened and remember a dream. Don't get frustrated, just keep doing the exercise.

### Step 2: Finding and Understanding Your Symbols

Dreams have a language of their own and there are many techniques you can use to learn to understand the language. In my opinion, dream books with generic definitions of symbols are not useful as everyone's symbols are their own, and except for a few universal symbols, will mean something different to each of us. It is a good idea then to begin to understand what each symbol means to you. For instance, what do you feel when you see a snake? Is the feeling different if the snake is just lying there compared to if it looks like it will strike at you? What do different colors represent? Is black good or bad? How about white? What meanings do you associate with different buildings: schools, libraries, jails? What about bodies of water: lakes, ocean, rivers, streams? These things may have very different meanings to me than to you.

List some of your symbols and record what they mean to you:

**Automobile:**

_____
_____
_____
_____

**Colors:**

_____
_____
_____
_____

**Forest:**

_____
_____
_____
_____

**Ocean:**

_____
_____
_____
_____

**Darkness:**

_____
_____
_____
_____

### Step 3: Interpretation

- ❖ First, read over the dream you recorded the night before, and as you are reading it, underline with a highlighter anything that seems to jump out at you.

- ❖ If the dream was a result of a question you asked before falling asleep, put the question at the top of the paper.

*Example:* **What should I do about my life?**

**Hypothetical Recorded Answer:**

I am at a **carnival** that is very bright and **chaotic, lots of noise**. I am on a merry-go-round **going in circles**. Next, I am in **a crowd that's pushing me in a direction that I don't want to go**. I am very **frustrated and angry**. I decide to go someplace quiet so I head to the **library**. It feels safe. It reminds me of **school** and how much I love to **learn**. I can breathe again.

**Interpretation:** I feel like my life is in chaos and that I am going in circles because I am allowing others to control me which makes me angry and frustrated. I need to feel like my life is safe. If I go back to school I can get control of my life again.

### *Thematic Approach to Interpretation*

Look for a theme instead of looking for a meaning from the symbols. Focus on verbs and turn nouns into generalizations as you also turn pronouns into someone and objects into something. Relationships between the parts are highlighted and the theme is related to your everyday life.

Example:

**Verbs:**

_____
_____
_____
_____
_____

**Nouns:**

_____
_____
_____
_____
_____

**Pronouns:**

_____
_____
_____
_____
_____

**Object(s):**

_____
_____
_____
_____

## How does it relate to your life?

## Interpretation using Thematic Approach:

## *Ego Approach to Interpretation:*

Ask yourself what you are doing in the dream and how it relates to your current life. What are you feeling? Are you in an active or passive role in the dream? Are you taking action or is something being done to you?

**What are you doing?**

**What are you feeling?**

**Active or passive?**

**Interpretation using Ego Approach:**

*Key Question Approach to Interpretation:*

Ask questions that are specific to the dream or explore its qualities. For example, did this dream make you feel happy, scared, anxious?

How did you respond?

**Why did you participate with the dream? For example, why did you have the conversation, argument, or feelings of anger?**

*Gestalt Dialoguing Technique for Interpretation:*

In this technique, you will actually talk to one of the characters or objects in your dream.

**On the following page,** ask a question and write the first thing that comes into your mind. Keep doing this until the dream becomes clearer and you believe you understand the dream's message.

**Here is an example** of a dream I personally experienced: *I was sitting in a running car, waiting to pull out into traffic. Out of the bushes jumped an old man wielding a knife. He began stabbing the closed car window. I remember being terrified.*

On first examination, the dream seems nonsensical because I was not in danger. The window was rolled up and the car was running so I could just drive off. However, I remember being very frightened in it. In my post dream dialogue, it would have been logical to talk with the man, but for some reason, I decided it was more important to dialogue with the knife. Here is the dialogue and the response:

"What are you?"

"I am your fears."

"What are you trying to tell me?"

"These fears are old and harmless. You have all the power. Let go of the past."

*It was the perfect explanation.*


**Ask a question to a person or object in your dream and write a dialogue about it:**

_____
_____
_____
_____
_____
_____
_____
_____
_____
_____
_____
_____
_____
_____
_____
_____
_____
_____
_____
_____

## Continuing the Dream—Active Imagination Technique for Interpretation

This works well with snippets of dreams and nightmares.

After you awaken and you look over the dream or snippet, continue it in your mind—daydream. This is especially effective with a nightmare as you can play it to a successful conclusion, taking the fear out of the dream. Write it out here:

# Possible Reasons for Dreams that Seem Very Different from Your Normal Dreaming

Could this dream actually be a conversation with a deceased loved one, angel or guide? What is the message? Explore these ideas in writing:

Could the dream be a past life memory? Attempt to ascertain when it took place and whether you are just an observer or a participant in the dream. Are the colors much brighter, more vivid? That is something that is often seen in past life dreams. Does it have absolutely no relevance to your current life or anything happening in it? Does it explain a phobia or physical problem you have that has no relationship to anything that has happened to you in this life? Explore these ideas in writing:

Is the dream precognitive, foreshadowing something to come? What is the warning? If relevant, write about this possibility:

It is important to answer these questions if the dream is unusual or feels different to you.

If you cannot come up with an interpretation, ask someone else, a friend or relative, someone who knows you well is best. You may be blocking because you really don't want to see what the dream is telling you.

## Step 5: Dream Journal:

I believe it is essential, especially in the beginning, to keep a dream journal. Write down all your dreams, including snippets of dreams. Make sure to date and leave plenty of space while writing so that you can mark up your journal with your interpretation. After three months, go back over your past dreams. Do they make more sense now? Has anything come true? Are you getting dreams that are solving problems or helping your creativity?

Looking at past dreams can also help you to see how far you are moving forward in your life and what your subconscious mind is trying to tell you.

## Step 6: Programming Dreams

Dreams are a wonderful way to communicate with guides and loved ones, to get information about what's going on in your subconscious mind, and to predict what might be coming in your life. They are also wonderful tools to get creative, problem-solving advice from the Universe.

The steps are simple. Prior to going to sleep, merely say that you desire a dream that helps you solve a specific problem, helps you design something you're having problems with, or gives you a missing puzzle piece.

Often you won't even need to ask. Many times we will have a dream that solves a dilemma. Elias Howe, the inventor of the sewing machine, had this experience. Howe was on the verge of bankruptcy when he had a dream about where the eye of the needle of the sewing machine should be located. "His original idea was to follow the model of the ordinary needle, and have the eye at the heel. It never occurred to him that it should be placed near the point, and he might have failed altogether if he had not dreamed he was building a sewing machine for a savage king in a strange country. Just as in his actual working experience, he was perplexed about the needle's eye. He thought the king gave him twenty-four hours in which to complete the machine and make it sew. If not finished in that time, death was to be the punishment. Howe worked and worked and puzzled and finally gave it up. Then he dreamed he was taken out to be executed. He noticed that the warriors carried spears that were pierced near the head. Instantly came the solution of the difficulty, and while the inventor was begging for time, he awoke. It was 4 o'clock in the morning. He jumped out of bed, ran to his workshop, and by 9 a.m., a needle with an eye at the point had been rudely modeled. After that it was easy." (wikipedia.org/wiki/Elias_Howe)

## Other Things Dreams Can Be Used For

- *Health*: often dreams will alert us to health problems.
- *Inner growth*: dreams can help you understand subconscious motivations and help with dialoguing with our guides, angels, and loved ones.
- *Creative problem solving*: Right before you go to sleep, think of a problem you are having trouble with in your life. Often a dream will give you new ideas which help create a solution.
- *Rehearsing*: dreams can help us deal with an upcoming frightening event by seeing the event clearly, working through the best way to accomplish something, practicing and releasing the fear through mastery.
- *Wish fulfillment and recreation:* sex dreams and dreams of flying, for example.

*"Dreams are today's answers to tomorrow's questions."*
Edgar Caycee, clairvoyant & channel

# LESSON 13

## LUCID DREAMING

**In a lucid dream,** you are aware that you are dreaming *and* you can manipulate the dream if you choose to. Many people claim to have had this experience at least once, but frequent lucid dreaming is rare.

Lucid dreaming occurs most often during REM sleep, usually as the last dream of the night. REM sleep is the most active state of sleep and when most dreams occur. Your heart rate and eye movements also increase.

There are several different methods for experiencing a lucid dream, but the first step is to become aware of when you are dreaming and to begin to keep a log of your dreams. This is best accomplished by keeping a dream journal, simply a notebook where you record, write out, your dreams.

### Techniques to Recognize Lucid Dreaming

*Reality Testing:*

Your level of consciousness is similar when you are awake or while you are dreaming. If you increase your awareness while awake, you will be more conscious of when you are dreaming.

Reality testing is a popular way to do this. Throughout the day you check in with your awareness as to whether you are awake or asleep. This trains your brain to recognize your dream states (i.e. imagined sensations that seem real) from your waking states. Ask yourself at different times of day whether you are awake or asleep. After a while, this will become a habit.

*Ways to Practice Reality Tests:*

~ Push your fingers against your opposite palm. If they pass through, you are dreaming.

~ Look frequently into mirrors during the day. In a dream state, your reflection will not look normal.

~ Pinch your nose closed. If you are asleep, you will still perceive yourself as breathing.

~ Look away from text of any books you are reading then look back again. If you are dreaming, the text will change.

~ If you have tattoos, look at them. They look different in a dream.

Just ask yourself, *Am I dreaming?* several times a day.

Find the test you like best and do it several times per day.


*Induction Techniques*:

While lucid dreaming often happens randomly, it's possible to initiate lucid dreaming through one of these induction techniques:

### WBTB: Wake Back to Bed
Set your alarm for 5 hours after bedtime. Go back to sleep. Often you will have a lucid dream due to immediately entering REM sleep while you are still somewhat conscious.

### MILD: Mnemonic Induction of Lucid Dreams
Tell yourself that you will lucid dream tonight. Do this often during the day and as you go to sleep that night.

### WILD: Wake-Initiated Lucid Dream
To initiate this technique you must enter REM sleep from a state of wakefulness while maintaining your consciousness. This involves lying down until you have a hypnagogic hallucination (a hallucination that seems real where you think you feel someone touching you or you hear sounds, for example).

To increase your chances of lucid dreaming, use these techniques with reality testing and dream journaling.

*The Benefits of Lucid Dreaming:*

**Can decrease nightmares** — While lucid dreaming, you can change the nightmare into a regular dream either by conquering the issue in the dream or changing the dream entirely. During a lucid dream, you can realize that the nightmare isn't real.

**Can relieve anxiety** — By decreasing nightmares, lucid dreaming may ease nightmare-related anxiety. It is also used to relieve anxiety due to PTSD.

**Can increase motor skills** — Visualizing physical movements can increase the actual ability to do them. This may be done during a lucid dream, where the dreamer can mentally practice motor skills. When you perform activities while dreaming, your brain's sensorimotor cortex activates. This is the part of the brain that controls movement so this activation can improve sports performance and other motor skills.

**Can enhance creativity** — Typically, people who are more creative are more likely to lucid dream. This might be due to their heightened ability to recall dreams and visualize events. But according to anecdotal reports, it also works the other way around. People claim lucid dreaming increases their creativity and imagination.

*Interpreting Lucid Dreams:*

In fact, people say dream interpretation is easier during a lucid dream. Your awareness increases your ability to observe the dream as it happens and the dreams are more vivid, which helps you remember the events and details.

*Possible Risks of Lucid Dreaming:*

Lucid dreaming is generally considered safe, but there are some risks for people with mental health disorders. These include:

**Sleep problems.** Since lucid dreaming techniques purposely interrupt sleep, getting enough sleep can be difficult. The risk is higher if you have a sleep disorder.

**Depression and anxiety.** Sleep issues can intensify depressive symptoms and anxiety.

**Derealization.** Lucid dreaming induction meshes reality and dreaming, possibly making it difficult to determine what is real.

**Dissociation.** The overlap of reality and dreaming can also cause disconnection from your surroundings or self.

# EXERCISE
### REMEMBER TO
## VISUALIZE WHITE LIGHT

Spend some time prior to sleeping thinking about doing something: a speech, asking for a raise, playing golf. When you find yourself sleeping, remind yourself that you are in your bed thinking about this.

How did it make you feel when you realized you were dreaming?

_____
_____
_____
_____
_____
_____
_____
_____
_____

Did you awaken or stay asleep? If you awakened, how did you feel when you woke up. Did you realize why you awakened?

_____
_____
_____
_____
_____
_____
_____

# LESSON 14

## ASTRAL PROJECTION OUT-OF-BODY EXPERIENCES (OBE)

**An out-of-body experience (OBE)** occurs when a person separates their astral or spirit body from their physical body, either spontaneously or with intent, allowing for exploration of the astral realm. The spirit body is still connected to the physical body by a silver cord and can return at any time. Metaphysically, the concept is based on the belief that we are energy inhabiting a physical body—the astral body. When you experience an OBE, you are allowing this energy to leave the enclosure of the body and travel.

The basis of astral projection is that you can, with practice, separate your astral body from your physical one. An important part of astral travel is believing that there is an astral body and that you can, in fact, separate it from the physical one. If you don't believe this, you'll find it very difficult to accomplish.

It is also imperative that you have the ability to deeply relax. Dr. John Palmer, Director of Research at the Rhine Research Center in Durham, North Carolina, claims that subjects capable of reaching the theta level state of the mind are most likely to be able to have OBEs. Reaching theta is accomplished by relaxing and clearing your mind to a point between alpha and delta, a deep trance or meditative state which is not sleep.

Being in good health and in a calm, relaxed state of mind, along with being able to use your will to create what you desire, are required to accomplish an OBE. It is easier if you have the ability to focus your concentration so that no intervening negative thoughts can usurp the willed action and your desire to accomplish the OBE.

### What Happens?

OBEs may begin by feeling a sense of paralysis, possibly followed by a humming or gushing sound in your ears, and a vibration throughout your body, not unlike a light electrical current accompanied by a feeling of either sinking or floating. At this point, you will either become frightened (and then most likely fail to have the OBE) or you will find your astral-self observing your physical-self lying on the bed. Usually at this point (until you get used to leaving your body) you will come back rather forcefully. Most people become frightened once they realize they have succeeded.

# REFLECTION

**What fears do you have that could stop you from succeeding?**

_____
_____
_____
_____
_____
_____
_____
_____
_____
_____
_____
_____
_____

**What do you believe astral projection is?**

_____
_____
_____
_____
_____
_____
_____
_____
_____
_____
_____
_____

**Why would you like to try to astral project?**

_____
_____
_____
_____
_____
_____
_____
_____
_____
_____
_____
_____
_____
_____
_____
_____
_____
_____
_____
_____
_____
_____

## Preparing for Your OBE Experiment:

~ Prepare a quiet, comfortable place where you will not be disturbed. A bedroom is optimal as long as you do not fall asleep. Dim the lights.

~ For some people, candles and incense add to the ambience.

~ Make sure you are in a comfortable position, either in an armchair, sofa, or bed. You want to be able to relax completely.

~ Give yourself the mental suggestion that you **will** have an out of body experience. **Believe that you will have one.** Be happy and excited about having an OBE. Any fear will prevent the experience.

~ Remove all jewelry. Dress loosely and comfortably. Darken the room. Cover your body for warmth.

# Steps:

**(It may be easier to record what follows, leaving space inbetween each step so you can do what you are directed.)**

1. Make yourself comfortable and breathe deeply, hold for 5 seconds and release slowly. Do this for several minutes.
2. Clinch your dominate fist. Hold it and count to 5, release. Repeat 2 or 3 times.
3. Repeat the procedure by clenching the dominate bicep muscle.
4. Repeat with the non-dominant fist.
5. Repeat with the non-dominant bicep.
6. Take a short break concentrating on the feeling of relaxation and inner warmth.
7. Repeat with the muscles of the forehead by either raising or furrowing eyebrows.
8. Repeat by closing and opening your eyes, if you are working with your eyes open.
9. Clench your jaw.
10. Take another short break and feel the relief and relaxation.
11. Tense and release your neck muscles by touching your chin to your chest.
12. Tense and release your shoulder muscles by arching them backward.
13. Repeat by pushing your shoulders forward.
14. Tighten and relax your stomach.
15. Repeat with the rectal muscle.
16. Repeat with the thighs.
17. Tense and relax the toes by curling them as tightly as you can.
18. Repeat by pulling your toes toward your body.
19. Tense and relax your dominant leg muscles.
20. Repeat with non-dominant leg.
21. Stop and try not to move. Focus your mind on your state of total relaxation.
22. Relax your mind by allowing it to drift like just before you fall asleep. Don't go to sleep.
23. Look with your closed eyes at the blackness ahead of you. You may begin to see patterns, colors, or pictures. Ignore them and deepen your relaxation until you have lost all awareness of your physical body and any sensory stimulation. This state is often easier to achieve right after you wake up in the morning or from a nap. Start the exercise before you move.

24. Give yourself the mental suggestion that you will remember all that occurs. Repeat this five times.
25. Enter into a state of vibration through deep relaxation by breathing deeply through a half-open mouth and concentrating on the void in front of you.

# REFLECTION

**What technique works best to help you most relax?**

_____
_____
_____
_____
_____
_____
_____
_____
_____
_____
_____
_____

**How can you develop a better awareness of how your body feels and reacts?**

_____
_____
_____
_____
_____
_____
_____
_____
_____
_____
_____
_____

**Techniques for leaving the body once you've reached the vibrational level:**

1. Feel a hole appear in your forehead and will your energy to begin to be released like smoke through this hole until you can look down on your reclining body.

2. Concentrate on seeing yourself looking very closely at a point on the ceiling; a ceiling light or fan perhaps, something above your body. Imagine what it looks like as completely as you can until you find yourself actually up there and looking at it.

3. Imagine that there is a rope or a bar right in front of you. See your hands, astral hands not your physical hands, reaching for and then grasping the rope or bar. When you can feel your hands around this object, use it to pull your astral body the rest of the way out.

# REFLECTION

**What other visualizations can you use to leave your body?**

### Things to Consider

The first few times you will be jerked back into your body out of shock or fear. There is nothing to fear as you cannot be disconnected from your body. I usually, however, keep a White Light of Protection around my body just to make sure that nothing outside my control can happen.

When you get better at leaving and staying out of your body, it is often a good idea to practice by constructing an exercise that is a sequence of events you wish to accomplish during your OBE. Visualize these events often before the OBE attempt. For example, the event might be walking into your mother's kitchen and discovering what she's cooking for dinner, or arranging with a friend to hide an object in a park near your home so that you can go there in your astral body and determine what was hidden. Both of these exercises will help to convince you whether you are truly accomplishing an astral event or whether you are dreaming.

# REFLECTION

**What other places can you go to test your OBE experience?**

___
___
___
___
___
___
___
___
___
___
___
___
___
___
___
___
___
___
___

**What other tests can you devise?**

Astral projection is a topic that engenders both fear and excitement in people. The idea that you can run around in the world or other dimensions without your body is enticing. It's not that surprising there are a lot of myths and misinformation circulating. One or the most popular myths is that if your silver cord—the tether to your body—is broken, you will die. This, like many other myths, is untrue. I still recommend surrounding yourself with protection, but not because you may get lost in the ethers. It's just good sense to always have protection when working with metaphysics.

# LESSON 15

# REMOTE VIEWING

**Remote viewing is a topic** that may be unfamiliar to many people. It involves using the unconscious mind to gain direct knowledge about inaccessible targets like people, places, things, or events in the past, present, or future. It was developed by the CIA and the U.S. military during the Cold War as a technique to infiltrate usually inaccessible places like the Kremlin in an attempt to gather information. If you're a fan of the hit television series *Stranger Things*, you've witnessed a fictionalized version of some of these efforts.

A remote viewing session begins with a "cue" or question that sets up what you are looking for. Perhaps the cue words would be a map of nuclear facilities in Russia. These cues may consist of anything from the world's next catastrophic event to locating lost car keys. To quote from a website called *Learn Remote Viewing*, "In remote viewing theory, everything in the universe exists as a pattern of information within the collective unconscious, or what is sometimes referred to as the 'Matrix.' Remote viewing simply allows you to tap into this phenomenon and to transfer a particular pattern to your conscious awareness."

To get started, remote viewing is structured as a set of formal stages which correspond to progressively deeper levels of awareness the viewer goes through as they gain greater contact with the object. This is done singularly. A typical description of these stages is as follows:

**Stage 1.** Perception of basic, overall nature of the site or target like "land," "structure," "water," or "event."

**Stage 2.** Basic sensory perceptions like tastes, sounds, colors, qualities of light, textures, and temperatures.

**Stage 3.** Perception of the site's or targets dimensional qualities, i.e., height, breadth, width, depth, angularity, curvature, density, etc. Sketching of viewer perceptions is an important aspect of this stage.

**Stage 4.** Perception of increasingly complex and abstract perceptions about the site or target.

**Stage 5.** Asking your inner consciousness questions which allows details of the target in greater detail.

**Stage 6.** Allows further sketching and three-dimensional modeling or sculpting of aspects of the site or target, while acquiring further qualitative information.

Extended Remote Viewing takes longer. In it, a viewer relaxes on a bed or other comfortable support, and tries to reach a deep meditative state. If possible, the room is darkened and soundproofed.

As the viewer reaches the edge of consciousness, a second person in the room, the monitor, begins the session with directions to the viewer to access the desired target. Once the viewer can describe elements of the correct target, the monitor quietly poses questions about the target. These questions may request details, purpose, appearance, construction, activities, or other target-related information. The monitor records or writes down the answers the viewer provides. After the session, the viewer makes additional notes about what was perceived, along with appropriate sketches or drawings.

## Exercises

- Have a friend concentrate on you for 20 minutes at a predetermined time of day. Make sure you do not know where the friend is or what they are doing; you only know the exact time your friend will be concentrating on you. At that same time, put yourself in a meditative state and concentrate on your friend. After the 20 minutes have elapsed, or whenever you begin to get feelings or pictures, begin writing them down or drawing what you see. Remember, you may pick up colors, moods, smells, sensations, pains, or tastes so write down or draw whatever you pick up. Don't discount anything—even a sneeze may indicate that your friend is near something you are allergic to. Check with your friend and find out how well you've done.

- Sometime during a specific week, have a friend place an object, something that the two of you have predetermined, somewhere unknown to you. At the end of that week, knowing that they've placed the object, concentrate on the object and write down or draw where you think it is. You can also try visualizing your friend with the object and see if you can accompany them while they put the object in the place they have chosen. Remember, time is an illusion, so even if the object was placed in the past, you can watch it as it is happening.

- ❖ Send your consciousness to a place you've never been: the Vatican, Paris, a Greek ruin, a Mayan temple. Record all that you see, sense, smell, hear, or taste. Go onto the internet, Google Earth, or whatever site works for you, and look at pictures of the spot. Compare your earlier impression with your later research.

# REFLECTION

**How do you feel about leaving your body?**

**What do you fear could go wrong?**

**Do you have a strong belief in heaven and hell? How could that effect the experience?**

# LESSON 16

# METAPHYSICAL TOOLS

### Introduction

**What are metaphysical tools?** Tools are anything that you choose to use as a focus of your intuitive energy. A tool may be a wand, a dowsing rod, a scrying bowl, a crystal ball, Tarot, a regular set of playing cards, or any of the variety of cards that are currently being sold for divining. In ancient times, the Northern tribes such as Vikings, used a tool known as Runes. Some ancient people used bones and others used smoke. Some Native American tribes used herbs and sweat lodges, while the Chinese have been using the *I Ching, The Book of Changes*, for centuries.

## TOOL ONE
## Pendulum

### What is a Pendulum?

Just as radios pick up information from unseen radio waves, the pendulum is a powerful antenna that receives information from the vibrations and energy waves emitted by people, places, thoughts, and things. Acting as a receiver and transmitter, the pendulum moves in different ways in response to questions. It creates a bridge between your intuitive mind and your logical one and opens doors to perceptions that you may be blocking in other ways.

A pendulum is a symmetrical, weighted object that hangs from a single chain or cord. It can be anything that swings: a necklace, a ribbon with a heavy needle or key attached, a fishing weight attached to a string. There can be objects on both ends of the pendulum, but one object must be heavier. This end is called the pointer. I prefer to make my own by taking a crystal pendant and suspending it on a chain with something to hold onto attached on the other end, usually a wire wrapped stone of some sort. You should avoid a pendulum that has an object that is magnetic or could become magnetized; the stone hematite, for example. Crystal pendulums work best for me as they are already infused with positive energy.

## Working with Pendulums.

It is important that you pick the right pendulum. You must like it and it must swing easily for you when you hold it.

After you've chosen the pendulum, **you need to cleanse it**. There are many ways to do this. Here is what I like to do:

- ❖ Mentally set the intention that you want to clear the pendulum of any residue that may have been left by anyone but you. Focus on clearing away any negative energy it may have picked up.

- ❖ Run the pendulum under hot then cold water.

- ❖ Put the pendulum in a potted plant overnight covered by soil, then put it in sunlight for the day.

- ❖ Continue to set your intention. What's most essential is your intention to cleanse it and that you keep seeing it clear, clean, and refreshed.

Now it's time to **attune it to your energy and connect it to your higher-self**.

- ❖ Hold the pendulum in your hand. Look at it and take three deep breaths.

- ❖ Ask that your guides and angels be present as you create a blessing and state your intent, "I ask that this pendulum relay answers from my higher-self/spirit at all times, unless I request otherwise. I also ask that all information be truthful and accurate and one-hundred-percent aligned with my highest good and the highest good of all."

- ❖ Grasp the end opposite the pointer with your dominant hand. How you grasp the non-weighted end varies, but the two most common ways are:

    ~ holding the end with your thumb and index finger, or

    ~ put the non-pointed end between your index and middle finger up against the webbing of your hand (this is my preference).

- ❖ Steady your hand as much as possible and hold it out from your body with room to swing freely. Propping your arm on a table while sitting works quite well. Now ask your pendulum to show you what it will do if the answer to your question is "yes." At this point, there should be some movement, either side to side or up and down. Say "thank you," stop the movement and ask what its movement will be if the answer is "no." There should be movement, but not the same movement as with the yes answer. If you ask a question and receive neither a yes or no movement, but instead the pendulum bobs and wiggles, that is what my "maybe" looks like. However, you can ask the pendulum to show you what it will do if the answer is "maybe" or "unsure."

Occasionally the pendulum will not move at all. This can mean several things: that the particular pendulum is not one that responds to your energy, it just doesn't want to answer your question right now, your question is unclear, or that you're too close to electrical equipment or something with high frequencies.

Keep working with it. Relax and have fun. Carry it with you. Get used to using it and help it get used to your particular energy. This is especially true if you are using a crystal pendulum. Everything takes some practice.

## Why and How Does a Pendulum Work?

When you begin by connecting your pendulum to your higher-self, what happens is that the answers go from your higher-self to your unconscious mind (which then causes the tiny movements in your wrist and hand that make the pendulum swing) and then to your conscious mind that sees which way the pendulum is swinging. So, when you use a pendulum, you are moving it unconsciously in response to the messages from your higher-self. Spirits do not move the pendulum for you. It is a spiritual exercise in that it comes from the spirit in you. It is not a "paranormal thing"—rather, it can be an opening for your soul to convey information directly to you.

If at any point you feel the pendulum is out of your control, *stop using it*. Cleanse it. Visualize it covered in White Light (as you should be whenever you are using it) and say the blessing and attunement again.

## Suggested Procedure for Using the Pendulum

Each time you work with your pendulum, quiet and center yourself first and internally ask that all the information that comes from working with it that day will be true and for the highest good of all concerned.

- ❖ Start by asking, "Is now a good time to ask about _____?" This establishes your readiness to do the work. If the answer is no, ask if there is a better time. Attempt to come up with a date by asking first about tomorrow, three days from now, next week. . . until you get an answer. Be sure to follow up!

- ❖ Next ask yourself, *Am I ready to receive this answer?* Is the question any of my business or am I invading anyone's privacy? If you are not absolutely sure about the answer to any of these questions, don't ask the pendulum. Remember, invading another person's privacy creates extremely bad karma.

- ❖ Try not to ask questions that begin with "should." Should is a judgment and usually involves guilt. It is not a yes or no question.

- ❖ Make sure your questions are succinct and as clear as possible. If there are several levels to the question the answer will be unclear. Instead, ask the layers one question at a time.

- ❖ Be willing to hear the answer even if you don't like it.

- ❖ Ask your questions in the now. The answer might be different in an hour, a week, or a year.

- ❖ Always remember this: *your question will be taken literally*. For example, "Can I eat this?" You may mean to ask if it's good for you, but taken literally, if you have a mouth and are able to chew and swallow, you can eat it, so the answer is yes. If you want to know if it's good for you, ask if it's good for you!

- ❖ It can be helpful to write down your question(s). This allows you to refine them for greater clarity. It will also help you stay on track and remember what you're asking about. If you have a series of questions, write them all down. If you're asking a lot of questions or digging through a lot of layers, also jot down the answers so you remember the details.

- ❖ When you're first learning, avoid extremely hard questions. You do not want to make any really big decisions based only the pendulum, especially if you are new to it and just developing your skills.

*Now comes the hardest part*: TRUST THE ANSWER YOU GET! If you ask the same question over and over, you will get contradictory answers. This leads to frustration and anger and can cause you to think that it doesn't work. Ask the question, receive the answer, and act on it. As results confirm your answers, you'll become more confident.

## Why Are My Answers Weird or Unreliable?

Many factors can influence your success and cause unclear answers. Sometimes a pendulum swing that's different from your *yes* and *no* means something, so explore that. Is the question unclear? Is there an option you haven't considered yet and need to continue with more questions? Does this mean it doesn't matter what you choose? Are you afraid to receive the answer? Are you "testing" the pendulum?

Ask your pendulum whether you are ready to receive the answer. Is the question clear enough? Am I being fooled? Ask the questions one at a time; wait for the answer before asking the next question. You may not need to ask more than one to know why you are not getting an answer.

Realize the answer you get today may change tomorrow. For instance, if you are ill, and you ask if this medication is good for this illness, in a month that may no longer be true. You may have built a resistance to it, your illness may be different at this point, or perhaps now you are taking something else in addition that is contraindicated with this medication.

If you are having trouble developing a clear question, ask if the question you're asking is phrased correctly. If you get a "no" rewrite the question until you get a "yes," then ask it exactly as it is written.

## Uses

Pendulums can be used to answer any yes or no question on any topic including the sex of a pregnant woman's child, test for allergies, the freshness of food or water, the presence of chemicals or pesticides, whether to purchase something. Whatever you can think of, it can answer!

It is wonderful for contacting your guides.

I have used them to pinpoint areas on maps to help find missing people, pets, or lost objects.

They can be used to dispel negative energy from a home, car, any location or person.

You can use them to search or dowse for anything. Commonly, people dowse for water, but I have seen them used to find lost treasure, gold or silver mines, leaks in irrigation systems, buried power lines, spirits, and any other energy.

They can be used for healing or ascertaining where in the body something may be wrong.

Their uses are endless if you use your imagination.

# REFLECTION

**How might you use a pendulum?**

_____
_____
_____
_____

## Pitfalls

While a pendulum is a great way to get answers, you must also be aware of some pitfalls you may encounter.

- ❖ If the answer is personally important to you (your child's illness, the next step in your job search, should you buy the house you just fell in love with?), feelings of stress or desire can influence your ability to receive a clear answer.

- ❖ Keep your ego out of it and be open to receiving whatever answer comes without having too strong a desire for the outcome, otherwise, you could skew the results.

- ❖ If you have already decided what you want to do and you're asking the pendulum to confirm it for you, you'll get the answer you want, not what might be the *true* answer.

- ❖ Don't play games with it. After a while, it will begin to play games with you, too, and then it will be unreliable until your guides and higher-self again believe you are serious about working with it as a tool for true spiritual guidance. I also advise that you not become dependent on it. Too many people use them for everything and I believe it stops them from finding other ways to hear their guides.

❖ If you are ill, distressed, or your energy is way out of balance, the answers could be skewed. Be rested, fed, healthy, and in the right frame of mind before working with the pendulum.

# REFLECTION

**How could you sabotage reaching your higher self?**

**What other uses can you come up with for your pendulum?**

**Questions to Ask:**

1.

2.

3.

4.

5.

6.

## Answers You Received:

1.

2.

3.

4.

5.

6.

**Accuracy: Record relevant information documenting what transpired a month after asking the question:**

1.

2.

3.

4.

5.

6.

**How can you improve your skills with the pendulum?**

Pendulums, like Ouija boards, are enticing things, especially to teens. People have become dependent on them, not making a decision without consulting one first. I stress to my clients that anything you become dependent on is not beneficial. Pendulums are a great tool, but they are just a tool, one of many available.

If this tool doesn't work for you—and nothing works for everyone—try exploring tarot cards, astrology, numerology, or scrying (using a crystal ball to foretell the future), tools covered in the following pages of this workbook.

# TOOL TWO
# Crystals

Throughout history, clear quartz crystals have been valued by nearly every civilization. Theories exist that the great civilization Atlantis was powered by quartz crystal that harnessed and refracted the power of the sun. Other groups including Native tribes, African tribes, ancient Egyptians, Aztecs, Romans, and Scottish clans, for example, are said to have used clear quartz in diagnostic healing, meditations, and spiritual development. Crystals have been used as religious objects, in funeral rites, to dispel evil, and as magical enchantments.

Purported to resonate at the level of an individual's needs, quartz is believed to amplify whatever energy or intent is programmed into it and continues to broadcast that energy throughout the world and into the etheric realms. It is believed by many cultures and most metaphysicians that the use of crystals may accelerate the fulfillment of one's prayers, intensify healing or spiritual growth, or simply allow the crystal to hold a pattern of energy long enough and strongly enough for the manifestation of a goal to occur.

Crystals come in many shapes, sizes, and colors and they don't always need to be quartz. However, clear quartz is the most widely used.

## Different Shapes and Uses of Quartz Crystals

This will be a limited account of the crystals most commonly used as there are hundreds of sites on the internet that discuss thousands of types of crystals and their purported uses. In general, crystals are formed when liquids cool and start to harden, as in the case of magma turning to rock. Crystals have smooth, flat surfaces called facets that can form into geometric shapes. Metaphysical practitioners believe there are different purposes attached to particular crystal formations:

*Generator crystals* are crystals terminating in six facets, all coming to a near-perfect point at the top-center of the crystal. They increase energy, act as a focus for your intent, and offer protection.

*Channeling crystals* are crystals with one large flat face and seven smaller faces surrounding the larger one, all terminating in a point. They are said to promote contact with guides, extra-terrestrials and interdimensional beings, as well as helping make contact with your higher self.

*Double terminated* crystals have a natural point at both ends. Double terminated crystals are useful in any application in which you want the energy to flow in both directions. I like using them in wands and for healing.

*Tabby* crystal is easily recognized because it is a flat crystal, usually with etching or striations on one side. If the width is not at least twice the thickness, it isn't a tabby. They are said to be high frequency crystals which can help with communication and information retrieval. It is supposed to be very useful when attempting to develop psychic abilities.

*Record keepers* according to *Kacha Stones*, ". . .are crystals which have a small pyramid-shaped marking on one or more facets. It is considered a crystal within which wisdom is stored. It is thought that when one properly attunes with this crystal, the ancient knowledge and profound secrets of the universe can be psychically retrieved. They have been consciously and purposefully programmed by the beings who created the energies which have culminated in the actualization of life on this plane, and by their direct descendants [e.g., the Atlanteans and Lemurians]." (wkacha-stones.com) They can be any shape or type of crystal.

*Rainbow crystal* is any crystal in which a fracture has occurred creating a rainbow within it. Crystals containing these internal fractures have certain prismatic effects which produce powerful rainbows within the crystal, giving additional energy to the stone. They can be used as a powerful focus for your attention and also to heal all the chakras.

*Laser crystals* are a relatively long, slender crystal. They are an excellent crystal for developing focus, especially for meditation and intuition. They make powerful wands, and being quartz, naturally resonate with the intention of the user.

*Crystal clusters* are crystals grouped on a common base with many individual points. Where there is no base, the crystals bridge together. These wonderful healing crystals encourage a sense of community, creating harmony and removing negativity from the environment. They can also help groups of people to work together.

*Fairy clusters* are extremely fine, delicate, bright crystals also grouped on a common base. It is said that their frequency lifts the consciousness exactly the right amount to help those sensitive enough to perceive the fairy people. They appear to emit "fairy energy" because their structural refinement resonates with that plane. Their slender crystals are usually lasers, so they also share the properties of that formation. In chakra healing, they cleanse and dissipate unwanted energies and have a special resonance with the crown chakra.

It is also believed that other stones and other colors of crystals such as amethyst, tourmaline, smoky quartz, for example, also have additional healing properties and uses.

## Caring for Crystals

Crystals must be attuned to your energy and their new environment. This can be accomplished by holding the crystal and concentrating on it for a period until you feel it connecting with you. If it is small enough to carry on you, wear it or place it in your pocket and keep it with you for a day or two.

Some people attune their crystals by putting them under their pillow while they sleep or near their bedside. I can't do that as the crystal energy keeps me from sleeping.

It is also important to cleanse your crystal regularly because they retain energy, both positive and negative.

*Cleansing methods:*

- ❖ Place your crystal in a sunny window for a day or two.

- ❖ If it is very badly in need of cleansing, put your crystal in the window in a sea salt bath. Don't forget to rinse it thoroughly and don't do this if your crystal is in metal like a wand, necklace, or tool, as the salt will corrode the metal.

- ❖ Use your breath. Visualize your breath blowing out anything negative from the interior of the crystal. Put it at mouth level and blow hard. This is a great emergency cleanse if you are away from home and need to cleanse it.

## Exercises
## Focus Point for Meditating & Other Uses

- ❖ When you are meditating, use your crystal as a focus point. This is easier if there is a rainbow in it. Stare into the crystal with the intent that information will flow to you from the crystal. Continue to stare until you must close your eyes. Pay attention to whatever comes into your mind.

- ❖ Use your crystal for healing as they are excellent for adding energy. There are specific healing practices that can be learned from crystal healing practitioners if you are interested in further information.

- ❖ Add a crystal to your pendulum. Crystals increase energy and facilitate contact with guides as well as work with God energy. A crystal pendulum is more likely to bring truthful answers.

- ❖ Use crystals to balance the energy of a group of people attempting to work together. Clusters and double terminated crystals are best for this.

- ❖ Use crystals to keep negative energy out of a person, place, or thing and to balance the energy that is there. I keep a crystal on my computers and printers. Since I've started doing this, I find that I have less trouble with them.

- ❖ Use crystals to help plants grow. Put a crystal in the dirt taking care not to hurt the plant's roots and the plant will thrive.

- ❖ Use crystals to protect your pet. Put a crystal on your animal's collar and they will stay healthier.

# MEDITATION

BEFORE YOU BEGIN YOUR MEDIATION,
RECORD IT IN YOUR OWN VOICE.

Make yourself comfortable. Breathe while focusing your full attention on a crystal that is sitting on the table directly in front of you. Do not take your eyes from the crystal. Really look at it. Notice where the surface is smooth and where it is rough. Notice how many facets it has and where the light reflects from the surfaces. Where are the areas of the crystal that seem to draw you into it? How is it making you feel? Now pick it up, and holding it at eye level, stare deeply within it. What do you see? What do you hear, feel, sense? Is it cool or warm? Does it vibrate or move in your hand? Do you like how it feels? Continue to stare until you absolutely must close your eyes. Now what are you seeing, sensing, or feeling? Breathing deeply, feel your energy attuning, combining with the energy of this crystal, becoming one. Are you receiving any information? After you feel you are well attuned, begin your count back to this time and this space without breaking your link to your crystal. When you are wide awake, feeling wonderful, decide where the appropriate place for this crystal should be and place it there lovingly.

*Don't forget you now have a vital tool that can be used for many things. Use it often.*

Some people have a natural affinity for stones, crystals in particular. Many young children become fascinated with sparling rocks and some never grow out of that fascination. One of my clients was particularly gifted. During class I suggested that if you held a crystal in your hand you might feel tingling or warmth—some kind of sensation. After class, a student approached me and asked if it was normal to feel a crystal move. Opening her hand, she showed me a crystal in her flattened palm. Within seconds it began to move and literally crawl up her arm. To this day, I have never seen anything like it.

We all have certain areas where we excel. It takes trial and error, but if you don't give up or judge yourself by the success of others, you will find where you can thrive. This particular client worked wonders with crystals, that was her area of expertise.

# REFLECTION

**What color crystal resonates best with you?**


**What shape crystal seems to work best for you?**


**How do you relate to other stones aside from crystals? Do they seem as powerful to you? Research what the stone is used for. Does this make you more or less comfortable with it?**

# TOOL 3
# Numerology

Numerology is the study of numbers. It is an ancient "occult science" that originated from the Jewish book of mysticism, *The Kabbalah*, and was introduced to Western civilization by the Greek mathematician Pythagoras (569-470 B.C.). It is based on the concept that our world is energy and all energy holds a charge or vibration, including numbers. By learning and applying some relatively simple information, you can discover certain aptitudes and character traits of yourself or others. Much like decoding a secret message, a person's date of birth and name can be used to uncover information about that person. These numbers create potentials in life, both positive and negative. A person's numbers can help describe character traits, talents, stumbling blocks, life lessons, life purpose, and even motivations.

## How to Use Numerology

The first step in analyzing a person's numerology is to put together a "numerology chart." There are thirteen numbers used in constructing the chart. These numbers are 1, 2, 3, 4, 5, 6, 7, 8, 9, 11, 22, 33, and 44. To determine what numbers exist in a particular person's chart requires adding together the numbers of the birth date and the corresponding numbers of the letters of the full birth name. Remember you are working to achieve a single digit so always reduce the larger numbers until they appear as a single digit. This is accomplished by continuing to add together the number until it is a single digit. For example, 1949 would look like $1 + 9 + 4 + 9 = 23 = 2 + 3 = 5$. Each of these numbers represents different characteristics and ways of expressing those characteristics which will be explained shortly.

Every number that shows up in your chart has significance. Yet there are some numbers that have more significance than others. You may have numbers in your chart that are called "Master Numbers." The meanings behind these numbers are more powerful and can indicate that the soul expects more of you. Think of these challenges as opportunities for growth! You will know you have uncovered a Master Number if the individual numbers when added result in an 11, 22, 33 or 44. This is the only exception to the rule of reducing the larger numbers down to a single digit: *don't reduce these numbers*. They are reputedly intensified versions of the single digit numbers they replace: 2, 4, 6, and 8. When a person has these numbers in their charts, the soul is requiring more of the person; often that person feels compelled toward an achievement that benefits more than themselves. In general, people with

Master Numbers seem to have a potential for a high degree of learning and achievement. Many people find it hard to live up to the goals outlined by the Master Number potential and will instead use the number in its lowest vibrational octave. To put it simply, their soul may want the person living on earth to reach for the stars, but the instead, the person decides it's just too darn hard.

Before we get into the specifics about how to calculate the numbers, it is important to understand that there are five different calculations that I use in obtaining information. These calculations result in five core numbers which represent different facets of a person's life. One of the most important of these five numbers I call the "Birth Path." (If you look at other sources of information about numerology, you may see the term "Life Path." This is just a different name for the same concept.) This number represents what you are here to do. It reveals your most fulfilling direction and the major lessons you are here to learn. It gives a broad outline of the opportunities and challenges you will encounter and the personal traits that you can utilize to reach a positive conclusion of your journey. The positive aspects of the Birth Path number show the skills and abilities you possess, while the negative aspects of the number are traits you must learn to balance.

The second most relevant number in a chart is the "Destiny Number." (It is also called the "Expression Number.") It reveals your talents and abilities as well as many of your natural interests. It can show you the kind of career you will excel in and the opportunities and talents you have at your disposal.

*This lesson is not designed to be a comprehensive treatise on numerology.* There are, however, three additional calculations that are important. These numbers represent different facets of your personality. The "Heart's Desire Number" (sometimes labeled the "Soul Urge") reveals your desires at the very deepest level. Ultimately, it explains the reason for many of your actions. It is what you crave deep within your soul that often is unseen by others. The "Personality Number" (sometimes called the "Outer Number") is the face you show the world: your personality traits, how you dress and act in public. Your "Day Number" reveals your approach to reaching you Birth Path and, I believe, reveals how you see yourself.

The final core number is often called the "Reality" or as I prefer, the "Maturity Number." This number is not fully actualized until after we are at least 50-years-old, though it begins to be felt sometimes as early as 35. Your Maturity Number indicates an underlying wish or desire. It is an awakening as it points to the "true self" and your life's purpose. This latent goal begins to emerge as you gain a better understanding of yourself. With self-knowledge comes a greater awareness of who you are, what your true goals in life are, what direction you want to set for your life, and what you want your legacy to be. Sometimes the number will harmonize well with your other numbers, sometimes it will not. The Maturity Number has an underlying influence on our thoughts and actions later in life. It indicates your true power and your highest form of evolution.

## Using Abraham Lincoln as an Example to Calculate Numerology:

### *Lincoln's Birth Path:*

The best way to understand how to determine numerology is through the use of examples. Let's analyze the numerology of one of our greatest presidents, Abraham Lincoln. Lincoln was born on 2-12-1809. To figure out his Birth Path you would add together all the numbers, then reduce them to a single digit: $2 + 1 + 2 + 1 + 8 + 0 + 9 = 23$ which is reduced as $2 + 3 = 5$. We now know that President Lincoln has a 23/5 Birth Path Number. (I will explain the meaning of the numbers in the next chapter, for now we are just learning how to do the calculations.)

Mathematically, there are several equations to reach the number 5: $0 + 5$, $1 + 4$, or $2 + 3$. Some numerologists, myself included, believe it is beneficial to understand how the five was derived in order to get a clear picture of what type of 5 we are dealing with. We know from our Lincoln example that he is a 23/5. We can look to the meanings behind the individual numbers 2 and 3 to get an idea as to "what type of 5" Lincoln is; he must think of others first (a characteristic of the number 2) and be creative (a quality of the number 3) in how he chooses to act out his freedom (the goal of the number 5). On the other hand, if his 5 were reached by the numbers $1 + 4$, he would be concerned with using his own abilities (an attribute of the number 1) to feel secure enough (the influence of the number 4) to use his ability to act freely.

### *Lincoln's Destiny Number*:

To determine the remaining facets requires us to convert Lincoln's full birth name from letters to numbers. Each letter of the alphabet is represented by a number, one through nine. This table provides the conversion:

|   | 1 | 2 | 3 | 4 | 5 | 6 | 7 | 8 | 9 |
|---|---|---|---|---|---|---|---|---|---|
|   | A | B | C | D | E | F | G | H | I |
|   | J | K | L | M | N | O | P | Q | R |
|   | S | T | U | V | W | X | Y | Z |   |

In doing the conversion from letters to numbers, always consider the *full* birth name as it appears on the birth certificate, even if it was misspelled or the person was later adopted and given a new legal name. Any later change in name for any reason is not relevant; if a person changed their name after they married, the married name is not considered relevant. The only name that matters in Pythagorean Numerology is the full name as it appears on the person's birth certificate without using any name suffixes like Jr, Senior, or 2nd. I should point out that in our example, President Lincoln did not have a middle name. Therefore, based on the table, his full name converts to 1, 2, 9, 1, 8, 1, 4, 3, 9, 5, 3, 6, 3, 5.

To obtain the Destiny Number we simply add all the numbers together:

1+ 2+9+1+8+1+4+3+9+5+3+6+3+5= 60. Then reduce as 6+0 =6.

Thus, Lincoln has a 6 Destiny.

### *Lincoln's Heart's Desire Number:*

The Heart's Desire number is found by adding together all the vowels in the name until a single digit is found. The letter Y is considered a vowel if there is no vowel next to it and it is being used to represent a vowel. Admittedly, this can be much more difficult to ascertain with some spellings of foreign names.

Again, using the results we obtained from the letter to number conversion table, we find that "Abraham" has three vowels: the letter "a" which is represented by the number 1. "Lincoln" has two vowels: an "i" which is represented by the number 9, and the "o" which is represented by the number 6. We therefore calculate American's 16th president's Heart's Desire as: 1+1+1= 3 for the first name, and 9+6 = 15 for the last name. Then we add the two together: 3+15 = 18. Now reduce 18 as 1+8 to arrive at a Heart's Desire Number 9.

### *Lincoln's Personality Number:*

The Personality Number is based on the consonants in your name. As mentioned earlier, it has more to do with how others see you, your outer personality.

To obtain the Personality Number for Abraham Lincoln, we add the numbers from the consonants for his first name: 2+9 +8+ 4 =23, and his last name: 3+ 5+3+ 3+5 = 19. Add these together: 23 + 19 = 42. Reduce by adding 4+2 for a Personality Number of 6.

### *Lincoln's Maturity Number:*

At the time of Lincoln's death from an assassin's bullet, he was two months past his 56th birthday. Thus, we can assume his Maturity Number, which is typically in full-force by the time we are in our early 50s, was indeed actualized. To arrive at the Maturity Number, add the Birth Path Number with the Destiny Number and reduce to a single digit unless the result is a Master Number.

For Lincoln: Birth Path 5 + Destiny 6 = 11. This is a Master Number so it is not reduced but is written as 11/2.

### *Lincoln's Day Number:*

This final core number is the easiest to calculate. It is quite simply the day of birth. Therefore, Lincoln's Day Number is 12 which is broken down as 1 + 2 = 3. As you will learn later, in general, the number 3 means that a person is desirous of peace and harmony and needs balance.

## An Overview of What the Numbers Tell Us:

Now that you know how the numbers are derived, it's time to understand the meaning of the numbers. It must be understood that numbers have both positive and negative vibrations and a person can fluctuate to either extreme or be consistent. As humans we will rarely act only at our highest and best; we often act out the negative patterns of the numbers, too. If there is a Master Number to consider, the traits associated with that particular number, either positive or negative, will be more emphasized in that person.

*Here are keywords for each number:*

# KEY WORDS DESCRIPTOR:

### Number 1
*Positive traits*: individuality, self-starters, independent, original.
*Negative traits*: selfish, dependent, lazy, egotistical, self-absorbed, narcissist.

### Number 2
*Positive traits*: cooperative, good partners, balanced, mediator, peacemaker.
*Negative traits*: stubborn, codependent, worrier, indecisive, apathetic.

### Number 3
*Positive traits*: creative, communicative, peaceful, harmonious, effervescent.
*Negative traits*: moody, withdrawn, spoiled, superficial, frivolous, intolerant, manipulative.

### Number 4
*Positive traits*: planner, fixer, builder, practical, dependable, loyal.
*Negative traits*: stubborn, rigid, narrow-minded, oppressive, potentially violent.

### Number 5
*Positive traits*: exuberant, exciting, progressive, free spirit, great communicator.
*Negative traits*: lack of direction, sociopathic, irresponsible, sensualist, liar, manipulator.

### Number 6
*Positive traits*: nurturing, honest, responsible, idealistic, humanitarian, helpful, loyal.
*Negative traits*: martyr, depressive, critical, exaggeration, meddling, guilt.

### Number 7
*Positive traits*: analytical, observant, spiritual, hard worker, very caring.
*Negative traits*: pessimistic, dreamer, terrible with money, loner, sarcastic.

### Number 8
*Positive traits*: leadership, organized, ambitious, money creator, hard worker.
*Negative traits*: oppressive, bombastic, arrogant, obsessed with accumulating money and status, unemotional.

### Number 9
*Positive traits*: compassionate, idealistic, spiritual, humanitarian, non-prejudice.
*Negative traits*: easily depressed, worrier, escapist, dreamer, overly sensitive.

## **Putting It All Together**

One of the best ways to learn numerology is to put together the charts for many people, especially family members. This lets you use your own personal knowledge as a means to compare what the numbers indicate as well as give you additional insight into the person. Looking at the numerology of famous people can also provide a good learning experience. Let's take a look at a variety of people who share a common trait; a lifetime of living in the lime-light.

**Actress and Singer Miley Ray Cyrus**
**Date of Birth: 11-23-1992**

In determining Miley's Birth Path Number, we add together all the numbers of her birth date until a single digit is found:

1 + 1 + 2+3 + 1 +9 + 9 + 2 = 28 reduces to 10 reduces to a **1** Birth Path Number.

As we saw in the chapter on the Number 1 Birth Path, this is the number of the leader. The 1 creates independent individualists which Ms. Cyrus certainly has become. Now let's examine her other numbers to see how they might help or hinder her Birth Path Number.

Her full birth name, Miley Ray Cyrus, computes to a 68/14/5 Destiny Number, a 25/7 Heart's Desire Number and a 43/7 Personality number and 5 Day. As you can see, there are a lot of 5s in her numbers. The energy of the number 5 adds flair, creativity, spontaneity, and free spiritedness to the 1 independence. However, until the person is old enough to master their potential, an overabundance of a number can also increase that number's negative qualities. The number only indicates potentialities not definite outcomes. In general, possible negative aspects of the number 5 include: sensualist, irresponsibility, sociopathic and manipulative tendencies.

Other famous 1 Birth Paths: Tiger Woods, Steve Jobs, George Lucas, and Sting

### Entertainment Mogul Madonna Louise Ciccone
### Date of Birth: 8-16-1958

We compute Madonna's Birth Path as follows:
8 + 1 + 6 + 1 + 9 + 5 + 8 = 38 reduces to 11 reduces to **2** Birth Path Number.

When Madonna was just five-years-old, her mother died of breast cancer. Despite her young age, she had noticed changes in her mother's behavior, but she did not understand what was happening. Often "11/2 children" are quite intuitive and understand concepts without knowing how.

As stated earlier, the 11/2 can be quite introspective but can also become too self-critical and begin to feel out of place. In an interview conducted by Vanity Fair, Madonna revealed that she saw herself in her youth as a ". . .lonely girl who was searching for something. I cared about being good at something. I didn't shave my underarms and I didn't wear make-up like normal girls do. But I studied and I got good grades. . . I wanted to be somebody."

As is typical of many 11/2s, Madonna developed slowly, and at first was confused and without direction. This is partially due to her extremely high expectations of herself which certainly helped catapult her to later success. Additionally, her stage name, Madonna creates an 8 destiny number which added an ability to achieve goals and lead. As a highly competitive person, it became very important for her to attain success and have power. From the beginning, she ran her career like a business and continues to be successful.

Other famous 2 Birth Paths: Presidents Barack Obama and Bill Clinton, Vice-President Al Gore, Jennifer Aniston and Tim McGraw.

## Academy Award Winning Actress Alicia Christian (Jodie) Foster
## Date of Birth: 11-19-1962

Jodie Foster's Birth Path computation:
1 + 1 + 1 + 9 + 1 + 9 + 6 + 2 = 30 reduces to **3** Birth Path Number.

People with 3s in their numerology are often feminine, attractive, gentle children. Jodie Foster started her career at age three as a child model and two years later began acting in the television show *Mayberry RFD*. The number 3 often produces creative, optimistic, communicative, imaginative and sociable children. Not surprisingly, acting and modeling can be enticing careers.

With her 1 Birth Day adding independence and leadership, she, not surprisingly, expanded her creative skills by becoming a producer and director. Foster has a 5 Heart's Desire which adds a layer of risk-taking and adventure to her personality.

Other famous 3 Birth Paths include: Hillary Clinton, Alan Alda, Barbara Walters, Snoop Dog, Linda McCartney, and John Travolta.

## Media Mogul Oprah Gail Winfrey
## Date of Birth: 1-29-1954

Oprah Winfrey's Birth Path computation:
1 + 2 + 9 + 1 + 9 + 5 + 4 = 31 which reduces to a **4** Birth Path Number.

A person with the number 4 is likely to have traits of being steadfast, practical, organized, pragmatic, trustworthy, and determined; they are capable of producing anything through hard work. The Number 4 also relates to high morals, traditional values, honesty and integrity, inner-wisdom, security, self-control, loyalty, conscientiousness, reality and realistic values, stability and dignity.

Winfrey was born into poverty in rural Mississippi to a teenage, single mother. She has stated she was molested during her childhood and early teens and became pregnant, but that her baby died. After moving in with the man she calls her father, a barber in Tennessee, Winfrey landed a job in radio while still in high school and began co-anchoring the local evening news at the age of 19. Her emotional, ad-lib delivery eventually got her transferred to the daytime-talk-show arena, and after boosting a third-rated local Chicago talk show to first place, she launched her own production company and became internationally syndicated. She raised herself out of poverty and a desperate childhood as a result of her perseverance, determination, and hard work, eventually becoming one of the most successful women in the world.

Oprah's Birth Path Number 4 is enhanced by her Heart's Desire 4. This accentuated her deep desire for security and stability in her life. With an 11/2 Master Number Birth Day, Winfrey was fated to make her mark in the world; people with this number possess the potential to be a source of inspiration and illumination for others. Additionally, Winfrey has a 7 Destiny Number which can charge her Birth Path with brilliance, spirituality, intuition, and the ability to analyze and reason.

Other famous 4 Birth paths include: Arnold Schwarzenegger, Bono, Bill Gates, Elton John, and Jewell.

## Performer Michael Phillip (Mick) Jagger
## Date of Birth: 7-26-1943

Rolling Stones front man Mick Jagger's Birth Path computation is:
 $7 + 2 + 6 + 1 + 9 + 4 + 3 = 23$ which reduces to a **5** Birth Path Number.

Having the number 5 Birth Path adds flare, excitement, adventure, and the need for many and varied experiences. This is the person that must try everything at least once. No matter how wild these people are, no matter how many vices they may have, they usually come through their lives easily with very few ill effects. People like them and they love to be the center of attention.

However, with the 8 Birth Path, it is likely that Jagger needs to feel that he's in control of his life and his vocation. His career as the front man for the Rolling Stones is a good choice for him.

Jagger's numbers indicate he likes ease and is very creative: the Heart's Desire 3. And his Destiny 1 adds to his need to be a leader, independent, and unique.

Other famous 5 Birth Paths include: Steven Spielberg, Liv Tyler, Willie Nelson, Don Johnson, and Ron Howard.

**Singer Billie Eilish Pirate Baird O'Connell**
**Date of Birth: 12-18-2001**

The computation for this breakout musician is:
1 + 2 + 1 + 8 + 2+ 0 + 0 + 1 = 15
which reduces to a 6 Birth Path.

Six is the number that indicates potentials for family responsibility, nurturer, martyr, the champion of the downtrodden, intellectual creativity, discrimination, imagination, perfection, and the ability to use the imagination and the intellect in combination.

Billie Eilish is a singer, songwriter who exploded onto the music scene in 2015 with the song "Ocean Eyes" which was written by her brother. After just two weeks on the music platform Sound Cloud, it had been listened to several hundred thousand times. The next year, she signed her first recording contract with Apple records.

Eilish grew up in a close-knit family of actors and musicians and was homeschooled. Even with her profound success, she still lives with her family. An activist, she has fought for animal rights, veganism, and voting rights by working to register voters. She has talked publicly about her mental health challenges that began after an injury forced her quit dancing when she was 13. She found herself depressed, anxious, and suffered from body image issues that led her to become a cutter.

As a 6 Birth Path, she craves love and is very sensitive, especially to criticism. Family is very important to the 6 and having a supportive family has helped Eilish overcome much of her depressive disorder.

She is known to be a bit reclusive and to value her alone time. This is due to having both a 7 Hearts Desire and Destiny number.

Other famous 6 Birth Paths include: Albert Einstein, Eddy Murphy, Goldie Hawn, Jennifer Lawrence, and George W. Bush.

**Actor John (Johnny) Christopher Depp II**
**Date of Birth: 6-9-1963**

The computation for this world famous, if not infamous actor is:
6 + 9 + 1 + 9 + 6 + 3 = 34 which reduces to a 7 Birth Path

As a 7 Birth Path, Depp has numbers indicating tendencies to be the seeker, the thinker, the searcher of truth. The 7 doesn't take anything at face value—it is always trying to understand the underlying, hidden truths.

Sevens have an air of mystery and do not want others to know who they are. Intellectual, analytical, intuitive, reserved, a natural inclination toward spiritual subjects, aloof, loner, pessimistic, secretive, and insecure; these are some of the qualities of those born into the Seventh Life Path.

With a brilliant but unique mind, 7s often feel uncomfortable with school and Depp quit high school at age 15. Because of his need to grow and learn, he chose to experience as much of life as soon as possible and is quoted as saying, "I started smoking at 12, lost my virginity at 13, and did every kind of drug there was by 14. Pretty much any drug you can name, I've done it. I wouldn't say I was bad or malicious, I was just curious."

People with a 7 Birth Path are idealists that wish to live in an idealized world. They are often drawn to the outcasts of the world, often feeling they are outcasts themselves.

Because 7s can be loners or introverts, they are most comfortable by themselves. They can happily give up the stress and turmoil of a busy life in favor of a quiet, peaceful life of solitude. They value their independence and can find it difficult to relate to others especially in close personal relationships. Depp has been involved and married to several different women, but none have lasted long. With his 11/2 Destiny, Depp would desire closeness, even though it is hard to come by due to his natural solitary nature.

Other famous 7 Birth Paths include: George Bush Sr., Dr. Phil McGraw, Princess Diana, Mel Gibson, and Julia Roberts.

### Academy Award Winning Actress Elizabeth Rosemond Taylor
### Date of Birth: 2-27-1932

Actress Elizabeth Taylor's Birth Path is computed as:
$$2 + 2 + 7 + 1 + 9 + 3 + 2 = 26$$ reduces to an **8** Birth Path.

The 8 Birth Path is known for qualities that include strength as a leader as well as the capacity to accumulate great wealth despite ups and downs. They can inspire people. They can achieve powerful positions while also being stubborn, arrogant, and domineering. Arguably, Taylor's life included many of these traits.

Elizabeth Taylor began her acting career at the age of nine. By the time she was 12, her breakout role in the movie *National Velvet* made her one of the world's most popular teen stars. People with the number 8 Birth Path like control over their own lives, so it fits that despite being one of MGM's most bankable stars, Taylor wished to end her career when she was in her twenties. She resented the studio's control over her and disliked many of the films she was being assigned. Yet she continued to act, becoming the first actress to earn $1,000,000 for a movie role. She is considered one of the last major stars to have come out of the old Hollywood studio system.

In 2006, Taylor introduced a line of diamond and precious stone jewelry called "House of Taylor." The designs are said to be inspired by favorite pieces in her own collection. She actually wrote a book on jewelry and was considered to be an authority on the subject.

During an era where women's roles were very traditional, Taylor took on roles the represented powerful women not content to live the lives orchestrated for them. She has been labeled by some as one of modern society's first feminists.
Her stormy love-life is well known. She was married eight times, twice to her "soul mate" Richard Burton.

Taylor has a 9 Day Number. Traits often seen in this context include sensitivity, creativity, spiritual emphasis, idealism, and compassion. These different facets would certainly have helped her to play a variety of roles as an actress. Arguably, her most significant contribution, her desire to dedicate her life to helping AIDS-related charities and fundraisers, is consistent with the 9 Day Number working in cooperation with the 8 Birth Path. Her commitment to public service was significant. In addition to helping co-found the American Foundation for AIDS Research, Taylor formed her own foundation, the Elizabeth Taylor Aids Foundation with the purpose of providing direct services for people living with AIDS around the world.

With a 3 Destiny Number, Taylor perfectly imbued the qualities of the 3 Destiny; she was known for her beauty, creativity, and sensitivity. These qualities helped her to uplift and empower others.
Other famous 8 Birth Path include: Joni Mitchell, Richard Gere, Barbara Streisand, Victor Frankl, Faith Hill, and Stevie Nicks.

### Singer and actress Whitney Elizabeth Houston
### Date of Birth: 8–9–1963

The Birth Path of Whitney Houston's life is calculated as follows:
8 + 9 + 1 + 9 + 6 + 3 = 36 which reduces to a **9** Birth Path.

The number 9 Birth Path produces kind humanitarians, deeply concerned about the state of the world. Their compassion can cause them to be overly sensitive to anything negative and they will often feel guilty about things they could not possibly have caused or prevented. Because of this sensitivity, they need to live in a mellow, balanced, loving environment. Events even outside their immediate families, such as within their culture and the world, can deeply affect them.

Houston came from a middle class family filled with entertainers. Her mother was a backup singer for Elvis Presley. Singers Dionne Warwick and Dee Dee Warwick were her first cousins. Her godmother was pop singer and actress Darlene Love and her "honorary aunt" was rhythm and blues legend Aretha Franklin. At the age of 11, Houston began performing as a soloist in her church's junior gospel choir. At age 15, Houston sang background vocals for Chaka Khan and Lou Rawls. In the early 80s, Houston started working as a fashion model after a photographer saw her at Carnegie Hall singing with her mother. She appeared in Seventeen Magazine, one of the first women of color on the cover of the magazine. She was also featured in layouts in the pages of Glamour, Cosmopolitan, and Young Miss. Her looks and girl-next-door charm made her one of the most sought after teen models of that time.

Houston's debut album *Whitney Houston* was released in February of 1985. Rolling Stone magazine praised Houston, calling her "one of the most exciting new voices in years" while The New York Times called the album "an impressive, musically conservative showcase for an exceptional vocal talent." Her career soared and she even tried her hand at acting, staring with Kevin Costner in *The Body Guard*.

Despite her outward success, it is now evident how challenging Houston's personal life was. This is not uncommon for 9s; they often have difficult lives. Houston's situation was compounded by the fact she also had a 9 Birth Day. Her difficulties appeared to begin after her marriage to Bobby Brown in 1992. There were rumors of drug and physical abuse. Sadly, these are common problems for the very sensitive 9.

Additionally, Houston's 6 Destiny increased her sensitivity. It also explains why she could not easily pull herself away from difficult relationships. The 6 in this position increased her desire to be in a marriage, making her even more susceptible to staying or going back to an abusive relationship.

Other famous 9 Birth paths include: Elvis Presley, Bob Marley, Harrison Ford, Robin Williams, and Jimi Hendrix.

# REFLECTION

**How can using numerology help you in your daily life?**

**In what ways can you help others using numerology?**

**Is working with numbers comfortable or uncomfortable for you? If uncomfortable, how can you become relaxed enough to learn to use this well?**

# TOOL FOUR
# Runes:

Runes are most frequently stones imprinted with a symbol. They come in sets of 24 ancient alphabetic symbols. They can be made of different material: wood, flat stones, or glass being the most common. They are usually kept in a small pouch, bag, or box. They are readily available for purchase and should come with a book of instructions that explain how to do a reading and defines the meaning of the symbols.

In ancient times it was believed that the best way to cast, or toss the runes, was on an East-West axis facing the sun. Whatever procedure you decide is really up to you. It is traditional to lay down a white cloth (making the runes easy to see and in magical traditions, forms a magical boundary for the casting). Others cast the runes directly on the ground.

Before the casting, place your hand in the bag and stir the runes around. As with the use of any tool to gather information, surround yourself in White Light before beginning and set an intention for what you would like to accomplish.

Focus on your question and cast the runes—on the cloth, the ground—whatever surface you are using. Look at the rune to see if the symbol is right side up or reversed. Those that fall back side up are ignored.

For a quick reading, pick a stone at random from the bag and contemplate its answer. This is good for either a simple question or to forecast your current day. If you have a more complex question, you can reach into the rune bag and draw three runes, pulling them out one at a time and placing them in front of you. One way of interpreting these three runes is to think of the first one a general overview or representation of the issue you want addressed, the second rune tells you challenges and obstacles related to the issue, and the final rune shows possible courses of action you can take.

# EXERCISE

## REMEMBER TO
## VISUALIZE WHITE LIGHT

Ask yourself a question about something that will be occurring within the next week. For instance, how will this work or school week go? Write down the response exactly: the particular runes involved, the book interpretation, and your interpretation. At the end of the week, see how accurate it was and you were.

DATE: _____  Record the Rune response here:

_____
_____
_____
_____
_____
_____
_____
_____
_____
_____
_____
_____
_____

DATE: _____  How did your interpretation compare with the actual events?

_____
_____
_____
_____
_____
_____
_____
_____
_____
_____
_____
_____
_____

# TOOL FIVE
## Scrying: The Ancient Art of Revelation.

The word "scrying" means to reveal or perceive. Scrying in the context of metaphysics can incorporate several different tools, the common trait being that that they all have a reflective surface you can stare into. This practice can be done using water, a candle flame, a mirror, or a crystal ball. These tools are not used to predict the future. Instead, they let you tap into your unconscious and the unconscious of the cosmos. This is accomplished by complete focus on the reflective object or surface, like a mirror, in an effort to see objects or have a vision, for example.

## Water Scrying

*What you will need:*

- A black bowl

- Natural water: spring, mineral, artesian, or well water. (You do not want to use water from a public or municipal water supply).

- 1-2 candles

- Lighter or matches

- Small crystal object

- Flat surface

- A dark room

- Optional: Some scryers also like to use a smudge stick to cleanse the aura around them.


1. Prepare your bowl. Start by filling the bowl with water. Dark-colored bowls work best for aiding your concentration.

2. Place the crystal inside the bowl. Clear quartz crystals are best.

3. Smudge your area. This cleanses and purifies the area.

4. Darken the room.

5. Light the candles and place them next to the bowl with the light reflecting on the water's surface.

6. Enter a trance-like state by staring at the reflected light within the bowl. Continue looking into the bowl until you reach a state of focus, alertness, and peace. Focus on the crystal and the light reflecting off it until you receive a message or see something in the bowl. If your mind begins to wander, bring it back to the reflection.

7. Continue until you see something or you are too fatigued to go on.

It may take some time before you begin to allow your mind to perceive the images or messages. Do not get discouraged if it does not happen on your first try.

## Wands

Wands are most often used in healing but can also be used in spell casting. There are many different ways to use healing wands. You can use them to focus energy to certain body parts or use them to work with the whole body through the aura or chakras. This is done by scanning those areas looking for blockages and then directing healing energy to rebalance and unblock them. Wands can also be used to transfer energy via massage. If you massage the body with a wand made for that purpose, it will help to release tension and transfer healing energy to the parts of the body being massaged.

Wands can look like a long tube, often made of some type of metal, with a crystal on one end and a stone on the other. They can be made from a wooden stick that has been carved with symbols. Massage wands are usually made from stone and are smooth and rounded at one end. Many people add decorations to their wands such as feathers, beads, or carvings which are not necessarily for effect so much as for decoration.

### Wand Uses

~ For directing energy inward, use the smaller rounded end toward the body.

~ To draw energy out, use the widest point toward the body.

~ For massage on any body part for relief of tension or muscle knots.

~ To touch each chakra to instill energy flow and positivity.

~ Healing wands can gather and direct energy and transfer the energy of their crystal type.

~ To place on pressure points for reflexology.

~ To direct energy toward a goal or manifestation, and if there are crystals at both ends, what you send out will return to you.

# TOOL SIX
# Dowsing

Dowsing, which is also called divining or water witching, is an ancient method of finding things whether it is a lost object or person, water, oil, or metals. This is usually accomplished with the help of a "dowsing stick," a double-pronged stick or rods often made with a wire coat hanger or a pendulum

## How Does Dowsing Work?

No one is really sure how dowsing works, however some people theorize that some form of psychic energy connection is established between the dowser and whatever is being sought—an example of the energetic connection among all things. The dowser concentrates on the object they are looking for, creating a link with its energy which causes the rod to begin to move or vibrate. The dowsing tool may be acting as a kind of amplifier or antenna for tuning into the energy.

## Types of Dowsing

**Forked stick:** The method most often used is considered the traditional method which uses a small Y-shaped tree branch. Willow branches work well because it is a very supple wood. Holding the branch parallel to the ground, one hand at the end of each of the Y branches, the dowser then walks the area to be searched waiting for the stick to respond. When walking over the area that contains the object sought, the branch may respond by pointing downward, at the spot where the object might be found.

**Rods:** This consists of two L-shaped pieces of metal, one held in each hand parallel to the ground and each other. When the dowser comes upon the object to be found, the two pieces of metal will either swing apart or cross each other, telling the dowser that the object has been found.

**Map dowsing:** When map dowsing, a map of the area to be dowsed is employed along with a pendulum to help in the search. Holding the pendulum over the map, and when the pendulum begins to move in a predetermined way, the dowser knows they have found what they are seeking. This is an excellent way to look for lost people.

# EXERCISE

### REMEMBER TO
## VISUALIZE WHITE LIGHT

Make your own dowsing rod either with a stick, clothes hanger, or metal rod. Go outside with it and see if you can get it to tell you where you can find water on your property or public land.

How did you do?

_____
_____
_____
_____
_____
_____

How did you feel about doing this?

_____
_____
_____
_____
_____
_____

See if you can find metal on your property or a lost object in your home. Write down how you felt when you were successful or any feelings you had before any failures. Were you thinking positively about the pursuit or negatively?

_____
_____
_____
_____
_____
_____
_____
_____
_____
_____
_____
_____
_____
_____

# TOOL SEVEN
# Cartomancy

Cartomancy is the art of using a regular deck of playing cards as a tool for prediction. You do not need a special deck of divining cards to perform divination; a deck of ordinary playing cards works perfectly.

Each card in the deck carries a special meaning and it is that meaning combined with the other cards in the *spread*—how the cards are laid out—that gives you the answer to your question or questions. Although the meaning of the cards never changes, the way they are laid out can provide different ways of reading the cards. Some of the spreads are small—1, 2, or 3 cards—that are used to answer one question while others are larger and go into greater depth very much like different spreads used in Tarot.

What you look for in a spread primarily relies on two factors: the complexity of the question and the answer you are seeking. The more cards that are involved in a spread, the more insight you will receive about the situation. If the question is a simple one, a more complex spread may give you too much information and confuse the answer.

## Procedure

Before you begin to lay out the spread, shuffle the deck well while concentrating on the question. This will help the cards connect with you and absorb your energy. Once you have shuffled the cards, place the deck on the table in front of you. Cut the deck in half using your left hand and place the bottom portion on top of the top half. Now you are ready to begin dealing the cards with your right hand into the spread you have selected.

## A Few Spreads:

## One Card Cartomancy Spread

This is the most basic spread. This spread is exceptionally useful for a quick reading to answer a direct yes or no question.

The first step is to choose the criteria that will be used to determine your answer. For instance, "yes" would be a red card and "no" would be a black one, or even is "yes" and odd is "no."

If you want to look deeper into your answer, look to the card's meaning (which will be further explained) and you may get more information about the situation.

## Two Card Cartomancy Spread

These spreads can be useful when you are trying to decide between two choices. By using one card to represent each option, you can see the outcome of both choices to determine which one you would prefer. A two card spread can also be used to compare two different aspects of a situation, such as the past and the future, the positives versus the negatives, or two people's perspectives on a specific situation.

## Three Card Cartomancy Spread (and Sometimes Four)

From here on, the cards really start to tell a story. Now you will look at each card's individual meaning and start to investigate how the cards work with one another.

The most common three card spread is read from left to right with the cards representing the past, present, and future. Sometimes a fourth card is added to provide further insight into the future. In this four card spread, the third card would represent the near future and the fourth card would show the distant future.

The three card spread can easily be adapted to cover a wide variety of situations. For example, another commonly used layout uses the cards to represent the positives of the situation, the negatives, and a look at what is ahead. In a three card romantic spread, the first card represents your perspective, the second card shows your partner's perspective, and the last card gives information about the long term outlook for this partnership.

## Five Card Cartomancy Spread

This spread gives you a more in-depth look into the situation. Start by imagining the face of a clock, moving clockwise. Place the first card at 12 o'clock, the second at 3 o'clock, the third at 6 o'clock, and the fourth at 9 o'clock. The final card rests in the middle of the spread. The cards are then read in the order they were dealt. The four cards in the circle discuss the progression of events you are asking about. The fifth card serves as the climax: the final outcome.

## What Do the Suits Represent?

How the meanings of the different suits and cards was derived has been lost in history. The following is what has come down to us since playing cards were first introduced in the 14th century.

**Clubs represent action, passion, and inspiration**. They are associated with the element of fire.

**Ace of Clubs**: Spark of inspiration, passion. A new love affair, the idea for a business or life change.

**Two of Clubs**: Planning, delays, waiting for the signal to move.

**Three of Clubs**: You've done all you can, hard work pays off.

**Four of Clubs:** Celebration, rest, stability, pause.

**Five of Clubs:** Competition, petty arguments, fights, not working in harmony.

**Six of Clubs:** Success, victory, good exam results.

**Seven of Clubs:** Standing up for oneself. Defending your viewpoint.

**Eight of Clubs:** Events moving quickly, getting organized (fast), possible pregnancy.

**Nine of Clubs:** Stressed, but unbowed. Determined to finish the task/fight.

**Ten of Clubs:** Responsibilities, weighed down, burdened but almost at the end of the project/life stage.

**Jack/Knave of Clubs:** Feckless charmer. Passionate affair. Individual unable to focus on one task.

**Queen of Clubs:** Passionate, enthusiastic, fun. Career woman.

**King of Clubs:** Leader, always aware of the larger picture, not good at details.

**Hearts represent emotions, feelings, fulfillment, and of course, love and loss.** Hearts are associated with the element of water.

**Ace of Hearts:** New love, beginnings of a deep connection, conception.

**Two of Hearts:** Mutual attraction, love, friendship.

**Three of Hearts:** Celebration of friendship, a girls' (or boys') night out, end of an emotional cycle.

**Four of Hearts:** Emotional stability, possible low-level depression; unaware, or deliberately ignoring the positive aspects in life.

**Five of Hearts:** Loss, sadness, depression, grief.

**Six of Hearts:** Childhood, nostalgia, memories, the past revisited, an old flame appears.

**Seven of Hearts:** Feeling-based choices, indecision, going astray.

**Eight of Hearts:** Leaving, splitting up, change of direction.

**Nine of Hearts:** Fulfillment, understanding that solitariness is not loneliness, contentment.

**Ten of Hearts:** family, love, achievement of emotional peak.

**Jack/Knave of Hearts:** A person who is in love with being in love. Romantic suitor, short-term love affair.

**Queen of Hearts:** Someone to turn to; she offers emotional support, a listening ear. Watch out for darker undercurrents; she may have problems of her own.

**King of Hearts:** Kindly counselor, gives wise advice based on experience. Possible alcoholic or addict of some kind.

**Spades are connected to thought and communication.** It has to do with what we are thinking and our mental faculties. Its element is air.

**Ace of Spades:** Flash of insight, revelation, realization, understanding, idea.

**Two of Spades:** Reluctance/refusal to acknowledge the truth, withdrawal. Possible communication difficulties.

**Three of Spades**: Breakdown in communication; misunderstanding leading to a rift, fight, or break-up.

**Four of Spades**: Recovery, recuperation, time out.

**Five of Spades**: Deception, bullying, walking away from a disagreement. Resistance or nonresistance.

**Six of Spades:** Moving on, a change of direction, travel; putting the past behind you.

**Seven of Spades:** Theft, recovery of property or abstract quality (confidence, self-esteem, etc.). Subterfuge.

**Eight of Spades:** Feeling there is no choice, backing oneself into a corner, can't see the way out though the solution is right there in plain view.

**Nine of Spades:** Nightmares, repetitive thought, problems, anxiety, depression.

**Ten of Spades**: Endings, mental breakdown, the only way is up. New beginning.

**Jack/Knave of Spades:** Someone on a mission. Single-minded individual. Clever, sarcastic, intelligent.

**Queen of Spades:** Truth seeker, efficient person. She cannot put up with indecisiveness or stupidity.

**King of Spades:** Professional, good at his job, highly motivated and intelligent. Advisor, lawyer.

**Diamonds connect with the material word; all that we see and touch.** They cover such areas as money, work, practical projects, or homes, for example. Diamonds can also represent the practical aspects of relationships. Diamonds are associated with the element of earth.

**Ace of Diamonds:** Prize, gift, new home, new project, new job.

**Two of Diamonds:** Balancing the budget, time management. Juggling resources.

**Three of Diamonds:** Focus on work. Honing skills, teamwork, collaboration.

**Four of Diamonds**: Guarding resources, not socializing; holding oneself apart from society.

**Five of Diamonds:** Needing help, destitution, lack of money, loss of job.

**Six of Diamonds:** Charity, offering/receiving help, supporting another financially.

**Seven of Diamonds:** Materially well-off yet spiritually dissatisfied. Looking for a possible new direction.

**Eight of Diamonds:** New job, change of career, improving skills, undergoing training or teaching.

**Nine of Diamonds:** Material and spiritual independence. Satisfaction, happy in solitude.

**Ten of Diamonds:** Family, inheritance, traditions, family business, social gatherings.

**Jack/Knave of Diamonds:** Hard worker, loyal person, hidden attributes.

**Queen of Diamonds:** Home lover, nest-builder, mother, female leader.

**King of Diamonds:** Businessman, achievements through hard work. Enjoyment of luxury and fruits of own labor.

# EXERCISE

### REMEMBER TO
## VISUALIZE WHITE LIGHT

Practice card readings on as many friends as will let you. Practice makes perfect and will give you more confidence. Of course this is a tool you can use to obtain information for yourself, as well.

# LESSON 17

# SPIRITS, GHOSTS, POLTERGEISTS

**The existence of ghosts is a popular topic** in books, movies, and television shows. Non-physical entities do exist and sometimes interact with our three-dimensional world. Often, they are loved ones who have passed, trying to assure you that they are doing well. Other times, however, they can be spirits who have never completely crossed. They exist in a realm between our plane of existence and the Other Side. Many of these beings do not know they are dead and still feel all the pain and anger from the lives they lived. Some have been murdered, others were the murderers, while others may be suicides or very disturbed and violent beings. Understanding all the pros and cons of dealing with them is very important when considering developing your psychic abilities.

People who work with spirits are usually called mediums. A medium is a person who can contact entities both in the Lost Realm and the Other Side. A trance medium may also have the ability to allow those entities to speak through her or him by using the medium's body as a conduit, acting as a channel for the messages. You may also hear the term channeler which is different from a medium. I believe the difference is that most channelers seem to channel one entity or one group of entities consistently, whereas a trance medium's information comes mainly from deceased loved ones. Also, the entities vary depending on who is seeking the information: a relative, friend, or the police, for example.

There are many ways people can interact with spirits, but the most common way is via a haunting. Have you ever been in a house where one room or area was significantly colder than another? What about putting something down and watching it vanish then return minutes, hours, or days later. Have you ever heard footsteps, breathing, or felt someone sit on your bed when there is no one else in the house? If so, you have experienced a haunting. Hauntings can be short lived—a deceased loved one dropping by to let you know they are all right. Or they may go on for a long while if the spirit does not know it is dead or if it chooses to be troublesome.

# REFLECTION

**What "ghost experiences" have you had? Describe in detail.**

**How did the experience make you feel?**

**What did you do?**

_____

Some of the ways a house or area can become haunted are: a difficult or untimely death such as a murder or accident, family members refusing to release the deceased person, the spirit who has a strong connection to the place such as sacred ground to a native tribe, or the ghost refusing to realize it is dead.

The worst way to create a haunting is by literally creating the environment that calls to a spirit that has not transcended to the Other Side. This can be done by adolescents losing control of their intense energy at puberty. Searching for a feeling of power or just out of curiosity, they may be attracted to Ouija boards, satanic rituals, séances, or just calling on spirits or demons. These things can be dangerous no matter what your age, especially if you don't know what you are doing. In the hands of someone who lacks emotional maturity, it can be disastrous. Any form of metaphysical pursuit can be a spiritual journey of growth and discovery or a terrifying experience. But when you are dealing with spirits there are many more ways things can go wrong. If you are really interested in developing your psychic abilities, take classes if you can. Until you are older and have an established ego and sense of responsibility, stay away from things that can haunt you.

## Tips for Ridding a House of a Ghost

"Smudging" is a very effective way to cleanse an area. Essentially, a smudge ritual is performed to correct the energy in a home, office, object, or person. This is done by burning sage, or sage and a combination of herbs, in a focused, intentional way to cleanse out negative energy and to replenish positive energy.

When ridding a house of negativity, you must first open all the windows and doors, put sea salt in all the corners of the area that feel like it has the most activity, place a pure-white pillar candle in a bowl that contains water sprinkled with sea salt in the middle of the house, light it, then walk through the house with a burning smudge stick declaring your intention in a positive, firm way. Here is my mantra:

> "This house is protected with God's White Light of Protection. If you are not of God, you are not welcome here. I am releasing all negative energy inhabiting this house and grounds. I release all spirits and tell them to transition to the Other Side. You are dead and no longer belong in this realm nor are you welcome here. Leave now!"

Let the candle burn all the way out before shutting the windows. If you are religious, use a holy candle or a candle sprinkled with holy water and carry a cross with you as you walk.

The most important things to remember are that you must believe this will work, everyone in the house must want the spirit to leave, and you must make sure you never call it back by talking about or to it while in the house.

If this technique does not work, you may need to call someone, a psychic, ghost hunter, or priest to help you.

# REFLECTION

## Examining your feelings about ghosts, spirits, poltergeists:

**Do you "believe in ghosts?"**

**Do you believe they can be malevolent?**

**Have you ever been in a haunted house or area? How did you know it was haunted?**

## What is your belief about life after death?

## How might this belief color your interaction with spirits?

This is another topic that is filled with myth and fear. Most of what you have seen or read, especially those things that are frightening, are also not true. Keep yourself protected no matter if you are dealing with spirits or going to the grocery store. It's just good sense. If you really believe in your protections, you should be safe.

Teens, because of their fearlessness and recklessness, can create negative energy or draw-in low spirits. This is more worrisome because teens have not fully developed their ego or emotional maturity which can make them more vulnerable to a spirit remaining around them. Additionally, if the teen is wounded and angry they may want this negative energy around them; it makes them feel powerful. It can also make them dangerous. A teen, at the height of their most powerful psychic and hormonal energy surge, should be extremely cautious.

Sexually abused children that vacate their bodies during the abuse have been known to accept spirits into them. Just as a channel allows an entity to use their body, the child projects out leaving the body "unattended" which can create an opening. Because the child is so badly wounded and probably doesn't want to survive, the entity remains even when the child's ego returns. Now there are two beings inhabiting one body. This can happen multiple times with each spirit taking a role like the angry one, the protective one, the shy one, etc. I believe this is what happens in Multiple Personality Disorder. Studies done on people with MPD show that there are often both male and female personalities present, that the handwriting changes with each personality as does blood pressure and brain waves.

# LESSON 18
## HELPING A LOVED ONE TRANSITION TO THE OTHER SIDE

**Dying is a transition to another realm,** a better one if we let go of this one. If we are around someone struggling to let go, what I have found can help is to sit with them and give them permission to go; to let go and go to God, their loved ones, or even their pets. Just tell them it's okay and that their husband or wife, their sister or brother, mother or father, or whoever has gone before is waiting to take them over. Tell them to look for them. Help them to see them. Tell them to look for the light and within this light their loved ones stand. If they are quite religious, you can even mention that within this light Jesus waits for them; if they are only willing to walk toward it they will see. Just feel or visualize the person and in your mind, tell them the same thing. See them walking into the light. DON'T GO WITH THEM! If it's a child, having an animal come for them often helps. Don't be upset if they refuse to go. The tie to this plane of existence and fear of what lies on the Other Side is often greater than your assurances. Just keep working on it.

This works, too, if you are attempting to help someone already dead cross over. Spirits that are troubled when they die can refuse to go to the Other Side for multiple reasons. Often this is due to guilt or fear of being judged. In the case of children, it may be that they are afraid to go somewhere alone because they have been told not to leave their home, their family, or their neighborhood.

You can help these people transition, too. First, see if you can see them and envision the environment they have created. Often this will be the place they died. Assure them that they are dead and there is nothing more to be done but go to the Other Side. If they resist, attempt to figure out why they won't leave. They are usually quick to tell you. Reason with them just as you would a living person. Tell them there is nothing they can do from this place of limbo except re-experience their pain, but on the Other Side they will experience love without judgment and actually can help their loved ones at times. Attempt to walk them to The Light, but if they will not go, you may have to stop. Work with the family to send release to the person, then after a period of time, go back and try again. If the family has really released the person without resentment, pain, or anger, it should be easier. There are, however, some people who just won't go. Some because of fear, while others just do not want to release all the people and things they loved so much. Unfortunately, these people feel they have unfinished business and will not easily seek closure.

# REFLECTION

**What are your feelings about death?**

**What are your feelings about the process of dying?**

**How well do you handle change and loss? How might that effect how you help a family deal with their loss?**

**Did your religious training prepare you or cause conflict in you about death, dying, and the Other Side?**

**Who do you know that has a fear of dying? How can you help them?**

# LESSON 19

# CHANNELING & TRANCE WORK

**One evening in 1984 when I was holding a séance** in my living room for a group of students, a life-changing event occurred. Unbeknownst to me, two of my students, instead of invoking deceased loved ones as was our goal with the séance, had been asking for a "higher entity" to come through. Suddenly, one of the male members of our group began to shake uncontrollably. I reached out to give him support and the next thing I knew, I woke up lying on the table. My students told me that I had been "channeling" and that the entities that came through called themselves Equinoxx.

Channeling is an ancient practice that enables loved ones from the Other Side, guides, angels, arch angels, aliens—the list will vary according to beliefs—to communicate with those on this plane. The practice became well known in the late 1800s as the Spiritualist movement grew. Organized as a type of religion that continues today, Spiritualists believe that life continues after death and that the spirits of the departed can be contacted and spoken with.

Many mediums channel the same entity or entities repeatedly. This has been my experience as the exclusive channel for the combined consciousness Equinoxx (EQ, for short) for the last several decades. Every First Friday of the month for almost 40 years, I have opened my home for a public channeling. With the advent of the COVID-19 pandemic, we have successfully moved the channeling to online streaming, the date and time still the same.

I am an **unconscious channel** which means that my "ego" leaves my body. In fact, EQ refers to me as "the vehicle." I do not remember what is said during the channeling unless EQ specifically gives me that memory. I have been told that my left hand seems to become dominant (I am right handed) and that my aura changes to a different color. When I first began this work, I knew where I "went" during the channeling (studying with spiritual teachers, visiting with my deceased husband), but now I have no direct knowledge of where I go. I do communicate with Equinoxx directly outside of the channelings and they guide me in a mediation before each channeling.

People come to channelings to seek guidance, both personal and spiritual. Each channeler has their own way of conducting a channeling. During the course of an Equinoxx channeling, a Message to the World is given, then general questions submitted by the participants are randomly drawn and discussed. The questions are varied and serve to teach and enlighten those in attendance on such metaphysical topics as karma, reincarnation, spirit guides, and spirituality in general. EQ is a combined consciousness that claims to consist of representatives from all known planes, planets, and dimensions. They speak individually and some have highly amusing personalities but they always refer to themselves as "we," never "I." For more information about my channeling work and to register to attend a channeling, you can visit EQ's website: www.channelingeq.com.

## There Are Different Forms of Channeling

*In all cases,* the channel tunes into divine guidance from other realms and allows it to flow through them, whether through the words they speak, that which they create, or through healing energy coming through their hands or an object.

**Conscious channeling**: this occurs when the channeler is fully conscious and present, stepping aside to observe, and allowing a message to come through them. This can be from God, guides, loved ones, angels, or even from the person's unconscious mind. This approach is often used for doing readings.

**Unconscious channeling:** (As mentioned, this is what happens to me during Equinoxx channelings.) The channeler is no longer present in the body and instead allows the other entity or entities to fully utilize the body. Very frequently the unconscious channeler channels the same entity or entities over and over instead of entities connected to their client.

**Spiritual channeling:** can be either conscious or unconscious. These are people with specialized psychic abilities that have learned to receive information for others and interpret what the messages mean. They are not only the conduit for the message, but they explain what the spirit is attempting to convey through them. They usually provide general information about life, the spirit realm, and the human psyche.

**Trance medium:** these are often channelers that channel only departed loved ones.

**Physical mediums:** these are channels who work with a specific guide or guides to bring not only messages but sometimes physical manifestations like ectoplasm into the physical realm. They can also make sounds come through musical instruments, tip tables, create rapping noises, or cause things to float in the air.

**Automatic writing:** is a form of channeling in which you are either conscious or unconscious. In this form of channeling you find yourself writing material, either by hand or on a computer, that just seems to flow through you. You are not thinking about what to write or even what you are writing, but information is passing through you.

**Spontaneous channeling:** profound wisdom flows through you without conscious thought. This can happen in different ways and situations, the key is that the information is not something you would usually have in-depth knowledge of. For instance, you are having a conversation with a friend and what you say to them is exactly what they need to hear. It may be that they immediately understand without you thinking about your response.

**Creative channeling:** This is the ability to channel artwork, music, lyrics, poetry, sculpture, books, or anything else considered creative. Many authors claim that their characters are writing themselves.

**Energy channeling:** This type of channeling is used primarily for healing work. The channel becomes a conduit for healing energy.

## How Do You Know If You Are Opening to Channel?

✦ You have flashes of guidance and insight, inspiration, and higher wisdom that come out of nowhere.

✦ You easily find yourself dropping into a trancelike state of consciousness. You might find yourself staring and feel as though you are being pulled from your body.

✦ You have been intuitively tuning into some other entities since you were small, as a child you had "invisible friends" or spoke with animals or spirits.

✦ You find yourself losing time while being creative, and when you come back to the present moment, you have done a great deal of work without having a memory of doing it.

✦ You may instinctively find yourself offering guidance to others that truly helps them.

✝ Your daydreams are vivid and impactful, and when you come out of one, you have some important knowledge you didn't have before. This could be a solution to a problem, an invention, a new way of looking at a dilemma, or a deep spiritual insight.

✝ You experience feelings of deep peace and joy when you take time to be at peace or out in nature, feeling as though you are strongly connected to all things, and anything you need to know easily comes to you.

✝ You tap into profound wisdom beyond your current levels of understanding as you open yourself to your inner knowing, wisdom, healing, and a higher frequency that is beyond your usual state of being.

*When you truly are channeling, the energy and guidance flows effortlessly.* You feel elated, uplifted, and connected. In this trance-like state, time stands still and physical pain vanishes. You become part of all there is.

## Ways to Develop This Ability

✝ Become proficient at meditation. Be comfortable in the quiet and allow yourself to hear what may be coming to you in this state. Allow the knowledge to flow without thinking about it.

✝ Ask to become aware of when you are tuned in, and then believe what you are shown or feel.

✝ Work to keep raising your vibration. Think and meditate on love and light. Spend your days appreciating what is right and good in your life and practice gratitude.

✝ Record any thoughts that seem to come to you unplanned.

✝ Find a reputable teacher.

✝ Talk out loud to your guides and listen for their answers.

✝ Do some automatic writing. Just sit down, begin to write, and let the words flow.

✝ Open your creativity. Let that energy begin to flow naturally and without direction.

# EXERCISE

## REMEMBER TO
## VISUALIZE WHITE LIGHT

**Try a Form of Channeling: Automatic Writing**

Sit in a comfortable spot with your hand resting on a piece of paper or in the space provided below, while holding a pen or pencil. State the intention of wanting to communicate with a guide or deceased loved one. Protect yourself with the White Light, then begin your breathing exercises to allow yourself to relax. Close your eyes and focus on your breathing. Relax yourself and just allow your mind to wander wherever it choses, paying no attention to your hand. You can do this in front of a computer, too, with your hands on the keyboard. Just breathe and relax and give it at least 15 minutes to see what happens. If you can't keep your mind off your hand, you can do this while sitting on a chair or a couch while watching television. Just have your hand on the paper while holding a pen.

# A FINAL NOTE
## THINGS TO CONSIDER

*Don't be too hard on yourself. Developing your metaphysical abilities takes practice.*

*Fear and logic can get in the way of anything you are trying to accomplish . The more you try to push past your fear, the more stubborn it can get. Examine it, love it, release it.*

*Never compare your progress with anyone else. We all learn differently. We each start at different places, have different aptitudes, fears, and abilities.*

In conclusion—*never forget that you are a creator*. This workbook has given you some tools to master your abilities. *What you do with these tools and abilities is still up to you.* My hope for writing this book is that you will choose to be one of the Light Workers of this world. I hope you will reach out and help others who may not yet know who they truly are. I hope you will strive to keep our beautiful home alive and well so that we and future generations will have a healthy planet to call our home.

You **are** a creator. What do you want to create?

Myama.

Joan L. Scibienski

# ABOUT THE AUTHOR

**Joan L. Scibienski** is a professional intuitive consultant, numerologist, and astrologer who has worked with thousands of clients for over 40 years. She has lectured and taught classes on psychic development and spiritual topics throughout the U.S., Canada, and parts of Europe. She holds degrees in nursing, psychology, and metaphysics.

Joan has also authored three fiction books: "The Ariana Series"—*Be the Light*, *Becoming the Light*, and *Fighting Darkness*. Through this series, she is attempting to educate the public on psychic phenomenon, spirituality, and helping our beautiful planet to thrive.

To learn more about Joan's work as an intuitive consultant and for a complete listing of all of her books: www.intuitivedirections.net

For more information about her channeling work of the combined consciousness Equnioxx: www.channelingeq.com

If you would like the opportunity to be one of Jonee's students and connect with like-minded spiritual seekers, please check out her membership website:

**The Circle Led by Joan Scibienksi.**
www.thecirclegrp.com